D1239407

PHILADELPHIA: 1776–2076

Kennikat Press

National University Publications

Interdisciplinary Urban Series

General Editor

Raymond A. Mohl

Florida Atlantic University

Edited by

DENNIS CLARK

PHILADELPHIA: 1776-2076
A Three Hundred Year View

The Contributors

John K. Alexander
Dennis Clark
Peter A. McGrath
Graham S. Finney

National University Publications
KENNIKAT PRESS // 1975
Port Washington, N. Y. // London

Manufactured in the United States of America

Published by
Kennikat Press Corp.
Port Washington, N.Y./London

Library of Congress Cataloging in Publication Data

Main entry under title:

Philadelphia, 1776–2076.

    (Interdisciplinary urban series) (National university publications)
    Bibliography: p.
    Includes index.
    1. Philadelphia—Addresses, essays, lectures.
I. Clark, Dennis, 1927-   II. Alexander, John K.
F158.3.P592   974.8'11   75-33645
ISBN 0-8046-9141-X

TO RICHARDSON DILWORTH,
Mayor of Philadelphia, 1956-1962,
who sought the good city

CONTENTS

PHILADELPHIA: 1776-2076

The old and the new (courtesy of the Office of the City
Representative, Philadelphia)

INTRODUCTION

The city is certainly one of the awesome surprises of American history. Nobody at the nation's beginning envisioned it in its swarming power. Nobody really planned for it, for the admirably neat and softly tinted neoclassic designs of L'Enfant and Benjamin Latrobe bore little relation to the agitated building that succeeded the colonial era. The city did not fit into the careful governmental devices contrived by Madison, Jefferson and Adams. But it grew, feeding on commerce, immigration and a relentless preoccupation with machines and the products of machines. Recovering from the surprise of having built mass cities that now dominate the nation's life, Americans have been faced with the problem of how to understand what they did. The scholarship that would recover for us the record of how the cities grew is still in its tender youth. We built in haste; we repent in study in the hope that we can obtain a knowledge that will keep us from past blunders and future confusion.

To review the history of such a city as Philadelphia is a task surpassing all but the most comprehensively applied scholarly resources. For more than two centuries the city has been richly alive with the deeds, thoughts and collective energies of tens of thousands of inhabitants. The four essays in this volume are attempts to address citizens of this Republic as the third century of our national life opens with the unsolved issues of our habits of urban settlement. The occasion of the Bicentennial of American independence will bring forth addresses to these citizens from many other quarters. The authors of the essays in this book believe that a review of the history of the city in which the Republic was founded would be deeply instructive to all who care about the fate of that Republic's ideas, institutions and people. That is why these essays have been assembled. They are not a history of the city, merely views of it at three crucial junctures and one leap into its future. We invite readers to a Bicentennial analysis of what Philadelphia has been and what it can be in the lives of free men.

INTRODUCTION

The fact that the four essays presented are separated from one another by a century should convince the reader of the populous sweep of the city's past. An attempt has been made to have the essays deal with themes that extend broadly through the panorama of Philadelphia history, but there is so much as yet untold about those centuries of experience of the city's people and institutions that the reader may well wish to seek more of the story. For this reason a brief but useful selection of suggested readings has been appended. The four essays themselves are somewhat like the illuminations and fireworks with which Americans have traditionally celebrated their independence. They illuminate for only a brief period, but they salute a momentous national drama that spans the nation's history.

In 1776 the city of Philadelphia with its more than 30,000 people was straining with the urgency of its democratic emergence. The tension between its egalitarian goals and the vested interests of its population agitated it profusely, and its attempts to create agencies to care for its citizens according to its new ideals were rife with frustration. By 1876 much of the egalitarian drama promised in the American Revolution had unfolded. The city celebrated in an unprecedented way its own endorsement of American success, even as that success struggled with rampant difficulties of industrial growth and urban services. The twentieth century's realism does not admit of the kind of celebration concocted in 1876. We are too enmeshed in our deficiencies in housing, schools and income to celebrate heedlessly. Perhaps this is the best trait in us: we insistently seek solutions that can be broadly applied. We still seek housing for the poor, decent schools for all, decent incomes and political expression and control. In the spirit of this democratic quest, the authors of these essays present their views of Philadelphia, a city that now counts its age in centuries, its citizens in millions, its hopes in an infinite faith in democratic responsibility.

Dennis Clark

"A YEAR . . . FAMED
IN THE ANNALS OF HISTORY"

Philadelphia in 1776

JOHN K. ALEXANDER

Northwest view of State House, 1778. Drawn by Charles W.
Peale (courtesy of the New York Historical Society, New
York City)

Philadelphia was a young city in 1776.[1] In fact the city still had something of a rural tone. In the right season, one could pick blackberries at the corner of Sixth and Chestnut and wild strawberries out Spruce between Seventh and Eighth. A female Philadelphian claimed a walk from the Delaware River to the Pennsylvania Hospital or the Almshouse located on Spruce between Tenth and Eleventh "was the business of an afternoon." Whatever time it took, once she reached the Almshouse—or Bettering House, as it was called—and faced north, she saw a "great apple orchard . . . very full of very large trees." The Potters' Burial ground, located west of Sixth Street below Walnut, where "strangers," the poor and blacks were often buried, was a pasture. Before and even after the Revolution, a horn was sounded each morning in Dock Street near Second. This served as a signal for the owners of cows to turn them over to the "cowherd [man]," who drove them to pasture for the day. Numerous ponds dotted the edges of the city. There frogs croaked in the summer and people skated in the winter.[2] In such ways, the Philadelphia of 1776 had what later generations would yearn and work for: a kind of urban-rural continuum.[3]

Despite these traces of a rural environment, Philadelphia in 1776 was unquestionably a "city . . . in a very flourishing state." Few would disagree with Lord Adam Gordon, who said "one will not hesitate to call it the first Town in America."[4] Certainly Philadelphians believed their city was the leading urban center on the North American continent. "Amnicolist," in 1772, when comparing the colonies to "our mother country," asserted that "London . . . is their capital, as Philadelphia is ours." And Benjamin Rush probably already believed, as he said in the 1780's, that Philadelphia was "the primum mobile" of the colonial cities.[5]

Philadelphians openly displayed pride in their colony and city. In January 1775 a writer in the *Pennsylvania Magazine* boldly asserted that "Degeneracy is here almost a useless word. Those who are conversant with Europe would be tempted to believe that even the air of the Atlantic disagrees with the constitution of foreign vices; if they survive the voyage, they either expire on their arrival, or linger away in an incurable consumption." It seemed clear that "a happy something in the climate of America," "disarmed" foreign vices "of all their power both of infection and attraction." Philadelphia was a shining example of such virtue, at least in the eyes of Alexander Graydon. He proclaimed that "of all the cities in the world, [colonial] Philadelphia was for its size, perhaps, one of the most peaceable and unwarlike."[6]

Colonial Philadelphia may not have been as nobly virtuous as some of her ardent boosters claimed. But she was indeed the largest colonial city in the British empire. In 1760 Philadelphia had slightly less than 3,000 dwelling houses and a population of almost 19,000. By 1769 there were 4,474 houses in the city and her population had grown to more than 28,000. Five years later the number of dwellings had increased to 5,340 and the city's inhabitants numbered over 33,000. No other British colonial city could match Philadelphia's rate of growth. No other British colonial city could match Philadelphia's size.[7]

Philadelphia's claim to colonial urban prominence rested on more than mere size. In 1774, 880 ships sailed into Philadelphia's harbor. Such numbers led William Allen, chief justice of Pennsylvania, to proclaim "We have . . . outstripped all the other Colonys in trade and all manner of improvement and by the continuance of such blessings we shall begin to be the wonder of the world, and soon rival considerable states in Europe." Rival states of Europe? Perhaps not. But in "America," Philadelphia reigned supreme. By the early 1770's, she was "the busiest port on the continent of North America." Philadelphia exported more cereals, cereal products and lumber products than any other colonial city. The city handled more tonnage than any other colonial port. At least in trade, Philadelphia was the "primum mobile" of colonial cities.[8]

By the 1770's Philadelphia was also the leading manufacturing center of the British New World. Because of her role in trade, the city rather naturally developed a thriving industry in the production of barrels, hogsheads and other containers for shipping various food stuffs. The city even exported the staves and heading needed to make barrels. There also existed a flourishing industry devoted to producing leather and leather goods.[9] And Nicholas Cresswell, in 1776, held that "they build as fine Ships here as any part of the World and with as great dispatch." Not all shared Cresswell's estimate of the quality of ships built in Philadelphia. But by 1774 no one could question that the city built more ships than any other colonial center.[10] Philadelphia's lead in manufacturing stemmed in part from the great variety of items produced. A glance at tax lists for Philadelphia gives one a sense of the multifarious nature of the city's manufacturing. As early as 1756, Philadelphia numbered among its citizens people engaged in the following lines of production: goldsmith, jeweller, silversmith, mustard maker, distiller, chair maker, hatter, brush maker, sadler, jack maker, gunsmith, windsor chair maker, oris weaver, chaise maker, block maker, instrument maker, upholsterer, bookbinder, brewer, potash maker, pewterer, brass founder, net maker, bonnet maker, saddle tree maker, dyer, buckle maker, sugar baker, miller, wool comber, stocking weaver, rope maker, nailer, soap boiler, collar maker, plane maker, chocolate grinder, button maker, last maker, clock maker, glew maker, comb maker and more.[11]

As visitors to Philadelphia sailed up the Delaware, they saw visual evidence of the city's commercial importance and great size. Sailing past Southwark, the southern part of the city, one could see ships being built. One could also see the ship building facilities of Kensington located north of the city. Nearing the heart of the city, one could see many wharves jutting into the Delaware to accommodate the multitude of vessels that frequented the port. A person with a good eye and sense of distance might have noted that the city stretched about two miles north and south along the river. This great length, however, was not matched by breadth. In 1776 Thomas Jefferson could describe his boarding house, at the southwest corner of Market and Seventh Streets, as "on the outskirts of town."[12]

Once on shore, one quickly gained an impression of the city. Some few might have agreed with Ambrose Serle that Philadelphia was "built mostly of Wood, with little or no Attention to Elegance."[13] But the more common view was that the city's houses were "most of them Brick, well-built, and very spacious." Certainly the Philadelphia of 1776 contained a number of imposing structures. The High Street market buildings were hardly elegant. But the markets were "raised upon pillars, and covered over a quarter of a mile in length" stretching from Front to Third Streets.[14] For the day, the size and bustle on market days made this early shopping area a significant urban feature that bespoke the needs of a large city. Wednesday and Saturdays, the market days, were truly notable. Young Solomon Drowne observed that on those days "the People swarm to the Market House[s] thicker than Flies to a Hogshead from which Sugar has been started."[15] Equally impressive in size if not in "swarm[ing]" was the new "Monster of a large stone Prison" at Sixth and Walnut.[16]

Philadelphia could also boast a number of structures described as having stylistic merit. Dr. Robert Honyman found the Pennsylvania Hospital "a large & neat brick building." The Almshouse, or House of Employment, he proclaimed to be "one of the principal Ornaments of this place, being a very pretty building, large and in good taste." Carpenter's Hall, the State House and Christ Church were also often applauded as clean, elegant edifices.[17]

GROWING PROBLEMS

The existence of such structures marked Philadelphia as a city of prestige. So did the existence of six newspapers and the only monthly magazine published in America.[18] But for the modern reader, perhaps the most suggestive comment on 1776 Philadelphia's urban status was given by young Mr. Drowne. He wrote his brother: "O Billy! I almost envy you your pleasant situation on Mendon's pleasant Hill, remote from Noise & Confusion. Here the thundering of Coaches, Chariots, Chaises, Waggons, Drays and the whole Fraternity of Noise almost continually assails our Ears."[19]

For all the vestiges of the rural, the bustle, noise, traffic, newspapers, manufacturing, shipping and urban edifices marked Philadelphia as a great urban center. Still, as Patrick M'Robert said, "the situation of the city is very pleasant." And Philadelphia could actually charm a visitor. John Adams was often critical of the city. But as he left the city in October 1774 believing "it is not very likely that I shall ever see this Part of the World again," he wrote in his diary: "Took our Departure . . . from the happy, the peaceful, the elegant, the hospitable, and polite City of Phyladelphia." Nicholas Cresswell too was often critical of parts of Philadelphia, but still he said this "is the most regular, neat and convenient city I ever was in. . . ."[20]

For all such praise, no one denied that Philadelphia had many problems. There was, as Drowne observed, what would later be called noise pollution. Even some of the rural aspects of the city added to this problem: the loud croaking of bullfrogs could be extremely annoying.[21] Of course, the city could do little about the noise problem. And Philadelphia's record of providing needed urban services was, by 1776, quite good. On the eve of independence, no city in colonial America could point to a better system of street lights. Still, if Dr. Honyman was right, the best lighting was not all that good. He noted "by the number of [street] Lamps I can easily judge that it is not extremely well lighted." Philadelphia's streets were considered the best paved in the colonies, although Dr. Honyman found the paving quite inferior to that of major British cities.[22] Her night watch—the colonial equivalent of the modern police force—was not large. But it too set "the colonial standard." Despite complaints, the city's pumps provided, for the day, an often applauded quality and quantity of water.[23]

Philadelphia's efforts to keep the city clean were less successful. Starting in 1765, the city government said it would enforce the law calling for garbage removal from paved streets, lanes and alleys.[24] But these claims were not matched by performance. In 1769 "Tom Trudge," who said he was a "poor fellow," noted that only "those streets, which are honoured with the residence of the gentry" were regularly cleaned. That was, he said, somewhat understandable since paving was unfairly laid down in areas where the "opulent merchants and gentry" lived. Thus in the "alleys and by-places" where the poor lived "the dung-cart never comes." One had to "wade" through the garbage in such places.[25] While Philadelphia as a whole was not a clean city, people agreed the outskirts of the city were the most offensive. Benjamin Rush decried the "ponds, and masses of putrid matter . . . in the suburbs of the city" that produced sickness "every autumn."[26] Considering this state of affairs, it is easy to understand why some Philadelphians called the city "filthy-dirty" rather than "Philadelphia."[27]

The problem of keeping the city clean reveals a basic flaw in the governmental structure of Philadelphia. William Penn had expected his "greene Country Towne" to develop from the Delaware to the Schuylkill Rivers between Vine and South Streets. Believing this, Penn chartered a city government only for that specific area.[28] But by 1776 the city as a living entity stretched past South into the district of Southwark and past Vine into the Northern Liberties. In 1762 Southwark was made into a separate governmental district. But the street supervisors, unlike those in the legally defined city of Philadelphia, were not authorized or directed to have paved streets cleaned. The Northern Liberties remained unincorporated well past 1776 and so its streets did not even have the care afforded those in Southwark.[29] Given this divided and often limited governmental authority, it is not surprising that Philadelphia was a rather dirty city. Nor is it surprising that the "environs" of the city—Southwark and the Northern Liberties—were the filthiest parts of the city. This divided governmental structure that helped retard the cleaning of colonial Philadelphia shows that the "modern" urban problem of cities spilling over legal boundaries is not so new.

One problem in colonial Philadelphia was so nagging, so compelling that a greater urban Philadelphia agency was created to deal with it. That problem was the poor. As Philadelphia grew, so did the number of persons needing public assistance. By the 1760's the situation was out of hand. In 1764 the Overseers of the Poor for the city of Philadelphia told the legislature that the poor "are of late years greatly increased, and become extremely burdensome." The city Almshouse was ridiculously overcrowded. A year later the overseers noted that only extensive private donations allowed them to pay for public relief. In addition, the settlement law was especially cumbersome. This law required the local governmental unit where a person lived to provide for them if they became poor. But in urban Philadelphia, place of legal settlement was not always easy to determine. Thus both time and public funds were spent in arguing over which set of overseers had to support a poor person. Something had to be done.[30]

The predicament of increasing numbers of poor persons, increasing costs of poor relief and divided governmental authority was met head on in 1766. The Philadelphia overseers, the managers of the Pennsylvania Hospital and the city grand jury all petitioned the legislature for the creation of a House of Employment. A number of arguments were presented. This institution, which would also serve as an Almshouse, would reduce the cost of poor relief by having the able-bodied poor manufacture goods in the house. And to prevent expensive, troublesome battles over place of legal settlement, a greater Philadelphia agency needed to be created.[31] The legislature agreed. In February 1766 the legislature enacted a law "for the Better Employment, Relief and Support of the Poor within the City of Philadelphia, the District of Southwark, the Townships of Moyamensing, and Passyunk, and the Northern Liberties." To meet these ends, the law established "The Contributors to the Relief and Employment of the Poor within the City of Philadelphia." To become a contributor, one had to donate at least £10 toward building the House of Employment. The contributors were authorized to build and run the house. The Overseers of the Poor from the various areas were retained. Now they would collect taxes, pay for removals of poor who lived outside the contributorship area and give outdoor relief to those in dire need of immediate aid. But the bulk of the tax monies was to go to the contributors to run the house.[32]

The creation of the contributorship and the House of Employment marked a bold attempt to conquer urban problems. The effort was far-sighted and progressive in recognizing that urban problems did not stop at the legal boundaries of the city. But this bold attempt failed. It failed for a number of reasons, two of which are illuminating for our examination. One prime cause of difficulties was that the "suburban" areas quickly came to believe that they paid more than they should under the new plan. In petition after petition, the "suburbs" argued it was grossly unfair to force them to pay for a building for the "Use and Ornament" of Philadelphia when the suburbs could maintain their own poor "in a far more plain and frugal manner."[33] A second reason for failure came from the belief that the poor who applied for public relief could support themselves. As a 1772 essayist noted, it was clear that the "pleasing Prospect" of the city's publicly maintained poor supporting themselves by labor had been a "chimerical" hope.[34] The managers of the House of Employment, in November, 1775, painted the grim facts. "Few are ever sent there [to the House], but such as [are], sick, naked[,] old and superanuated [sic] or helpless Infants." The cost of caring for the sick, clothing the naked, feeding and housing the poor more than offset the little such poor persons could produce. As the managers rhetorically asked: "Where now is to be the great profits of manufacturing, carried on only with such people[?]"[35] Thus as the number of poor increased, the cost of public poor relief went up. The Philadelphia of 1776 was, despite its House of Employment, sadly aware that it had not found an effective way to deal with urban poverty.

The failure of the contributorship illustrates three vital aspects of the Philadelphia of 1776. It reveals that there was no easy solution to the ever-increasing cost of public poor relief—to say nothing of the plight of the poor who did not receive public assistance. It shows how divided authority did make it hard, very hard, to deal with "urban" problems that crossed legal boundaries. Indeed, even in the unified Contributorship the city-"suburb" division remained. And it illustrates that creating an effective greater urban agency to tackle a complex urban problem was, at best, no easy task.

As visitors to Philadelphia admired the House of Employment, they probably did not realize the difficulties caused by divided government authority. But they quickly saw and realized that the city was divided by more than governmental structure. The housing of Philadelphia was, to a large extent, segregated along economic and class lines. Such divisions occurred because houses rented "according to their situation for trade and other conveniences." Since virtually all shops were located in the central part of the city, it is not surprising that the rent for a house in "a remote part of the city" was much lower than for a house in a "good situation."[36] As the managers of the House of Employment observed in 1768: "the poor settle more in the Suburbs where the Rents are lower than within the Limits of the City—."[37] Thus in the Philadelphia of 1776 the more prosperous citizens tended to live in the central part of the city, and the less affluent tended to live nearer the edges of the city. This housing pattern, which reverses the modern trend, stemmed from two facts. The Philadelphia of 1776 was a walking city. There was no mass transit; there was not even a cab service. Thus it was a real benefit to be housed near the center of commercial activity. Also the central part of the city was the cleanest, best-paved and best-lighted area of the city. Why live in the dingy, remote environs if you could afford to avoid them? And as "A Citizen," noting both cause and effect, said in 1772: "the environs of this city very much abound" with "abominable [tavern] houses."[38]

The distinction of class was even sharper in the manner of dress. The reminiscences gathered and analyzed by John Watson indicate that during the summer in the years before the Revolution, "poor labouring men wore ticklenberg linen for shirts, and striped ticken breeches." Tradesmen and workingmen "all" wore leather aprons; "dingy buckskin breeches, once yellow, and check shirts and a red flannel jacket was the common wear of most workingmen." For the more affluent, "laced ruffles, depending [sic] over the hand, was [sic] a mark of indispensable gentility. The coat and breeches were generally desirable of the same material—of 'broad cloth' for winter, and of silk camlet for summer." During the winter, as the "poor labouring man" trekked about in his "gray duroycoats," "Gentlemen" used muffets "for they then wore short sleeves to their coats purposely to display their fine linen and plaited shirt sleeves with their gold buttons and some-times laced ruffles." The economic position of women was also distinguish-able in the days before the Revolution, since "all hired women wore short gowns and petticoats of domestic fabric, and could be instantly known as such whenever seen abroad." The difference in clothing went right down to the ground because "before the Revolution no hired man or woman wore any shoes so fine as calf skin; that kind was the exclusive property of the gentry; the servants wore coarse neat's leather."[39] Thus it had seemed log-ical in 1760 to say of an escaped criminal that his clothes were "such as Servants commonly ware."[40]

Philadelphians of the day felt that some changes in clothing patterns were occurring. In January 1776, "Monitor" claimed that many Philadelphia women

are desirous to make a figure as fine Ladies, without any fortune to support their pretensions to so expensive a character. Silk stockings are the accus-tomed ornaments of the wealthy; and yet those who cannot afford to pur-chase a sufficient quantity, will wear them too, but with this unlucky dis-tinction, that they appear in use a long time after they should have undergone the purification of the laundress. When the same spot is visible on the instep for a whole fort-night, we may not uncharitably pronounce the wearer's stock of hose is small.[41]

In 1772 "Simplicius Honestus" had noted similar changes—unlaundered or not—when he railed against the increased wearing of luxury clothing. He maintained that "this pernicious distemper not only discovers itself in the people of high rank amongst us, but is infecting those of an inferior class."[42]

"Simplicius Honestus" was not the only Philadelphian dismayed by the seeming change in the style of dress. In 1774 "A Merchant" sent an item he had clipped from an English newspaper to the *Pennsylvania Journal.* It called for limiting by law what apprentices could wear. Their hats should be "only" of wool without any silk. Their shirts should not have ruffles, or any fine needle work. Their shoes should be only of neat's leather. In short, the "upstarts" should "once more be humbled."[43] These comments suggest that changes were occurring in mode of dress by 1776. But one could still, in most cases, readily gain a sense of a person's economic position by glancing at clothing.[44] Such distinctions in clothing, and in housing, are not at all surprising when one knows that in 1774, 10 percent of the taxpaying households of Philadelphia owned 89 percent of the taxable wealth.[45]

The Philadelphia that visitors saw in 1776 was, then, a city divided in many ways. Different governmental units cut and divided the truly functional city. The housing of the city was divided along class lines. Class division was evident in the clothes people wore. These divisions had existed before 1776 and the Philadelphia that visitors saw in that year was not too different from the Philadelphia of about 1770. But there was one fundamental difference: Philadelphia in 1776 was a city at war. And for Philadelphia and the British colonies in North America, 1776 was the year of decision.

CITY DIVIDED

The lives of cities as well as the people who live in them rarely change with dramatic flourishes at neat intervals from January 1 to December 31. So it was with Philadelphia in 1776. Then, too, some cities at some times are so much a part of state and national politics that their history is inextricably a part of problems and issues that transcend city boundaries. So it was with Philadelphia in 1776. The story of that year must begin at least in 1775, and it must be related to the question of independence for the British colonies in North America and of a new frame of government for Pennsylvania.

The long-smoldering dispute between Britain and her colonies affected all major colonial cities. Still, Philadelphia managed to escape the extreme, open and prolonged hostility and violence that often rocked New York and Boston.[46] As late as December 1774, a Philadelphia merchant defended the nonimportation agreement designed to soften British policy toward the colonies by saying: "You cannot blame us for entering into this agreement—we are already over head and ears in debt, and from the restrictions laid upon our trade we have no prospect of being able to pay you." Still, the merchant hastened to add "it gives us great pain to find ourselves so much vilified in most of your London papers.—We glory in our connections with Great Britain, and we challenge any part of his Majesty's dominions to vie with us in loyalty and affection to the illustrious House of Hanover. . . . No plots to subvert government have ever been heard of in our land; we teach our children loyalty to our King, with the same breath with which we teach them to love and prize their liberty."[47] The London merchant to whom these comments were addressed may have questioned such claims. In May 1774, Philadelphia had created a committee of correspondence to support Boston's and the colonies' resistance to English actions. The first Continental Congress had met in Carpenter's Hall from September to October 1774. A second such Congress was scheduled to meet in Philadelphia beginning May 10, 1775. By the end of 1774, a Committe of Inspection and Observation for the City and Liberties of Philadelphia was working to implement nonimportation of British goods.[48]

Of course, nonimportation and loyalty to the King were not incompatible and Philadelphia, in Alexander Graydon's eyes, remained "one of the most peaceable and unwarlike" cities of the world. As late as early March 1775, Dr. Honyman, who was in New York City, observed "the People here are much divided, & Party spirit is very high, contrary to what I found at Philadelphia where people only mind their business, but here nothing is heard of but Politics."[49] Then on April 19 the smoldering dispute flamed into open warfare at Concord and Lexington Green.

The events of April 19 shattered the relative political calm of Philadelphia. News of the fighting reached Philadelphia in the early evening of April 24, 1775. The word spread quickly. Notice was given for a public meeting to be held at the State House. The meeting began at four on April 25 and Christopher Marshall noted that "by computation" the crowd "amounted to eight thousand." This great mass meeting resolved to "associate together, to defend with arms their property, liberty and lives against all attempts to deprive them of it." The organization of military units began immediately.[50]

Solomon Drowne saw all this and marked the changed state of the city: "I thought it almost impossible they [Philadelphians] could be possessed of a martial Spirit; but now my judgment is reversed."[51] The Associators, as those pledged to bear arms were called, met on May 1 in the city wards to form into companies and to choose officers. Samuel Curwen, who did not like what he saw, arrived in the city on May 4 and remarked "the whole city seeming to be deep in congressional principles" in opposition to British actions. The mood and actions of Philadelphians seemed so clear that within twenty-four hours Curwen could say "the City throwing off her pacific aspects is forming military companies." Thirty-three military companies were "already full or nearly" full. All manner of Philadelphians, including many Quakers, "stand shoulder to shoulder forming so many patriotic bands to oppose . . . the progress and increase of parliamentary authority in America."[52] One Philadelphian, on May 6, claimed that the city "has turned out 4,000 men, 300 of whom are Quakers." Two days later another citizen went even further: "almost every man that can produce a firelock is . . . learning the military discipline, and I verily believe that at this moment there are 5,000 men under arms in this city."[53] Philadelphia had "all of Sudden" become an armed camp.[54]

In May 1775, it was not easy to resist this martial spirit. On the 7th, Marshall was pleased to write, "It's admirable to see the alteration of the Tory class in this place, since the account of the engagement in New England. Their language is quite softened. . . ." Indeed, "even many of the stiff Quakers" were no longer so sure that "all humble and dutiful obedience" to the King and English policy was required. Not all showed Marshall's enthusiasm for resistance, but it was difficult to voice such views. On May 16, Curwen observed: "Philadelphia is wholly American, strong friends to congressional measures; at least, no man is hardy enough to express a doubt of the feasibility of their projects." As late as June, John Morton asserted that "we are heartily united in one general cause, not one Tory dare shew his Face in opposition."[55]

In the early flurry of patriotism, as men gathered under arms, Philadelphians hurled boldly optimistic and defiant letters at England. April 3, 1775: "It will not do . . . to quarrel with us; we grow very strong here, we can do very well without you. . . . Our politicks are all settled, we now appear composed." April 28, 1775: "the parliament seem determined to force us into an acknowledgment of their supremacy . . . I am sure they never can do it." July 4, 1775: "The whole of this city and Colony are resolute to a man, to oppose the invasion of our liberties; and are determined to lose our lives, sooner than consent to the least abatement of the privileges granted us, by a graciously provident God in our charters." July 5, 1775: "The sword is now drawn, and the best blood of the colonies will flow to support their cause; it is in vain you attempt a conquest by force of arms; you may ruin the fortunes, but you can never reduce the spirits of Americans."[56]

Logic decreed such rhetoric. Bold words might bring concessions, but outbursts of the martial spirit were soon tempered by reality. Even in the flush days of May 1775, some vexing issues could not be ignored. A writer noted that the Pennsylvania Assembly had been asked to provide £50,000 or £60,000 "for public uses." This was necessary, "for when trade is stopped, there must be means to employ the poor, as they must be supported." In July, "Business" was "at a total stand." By late September, "the great number of labouring people [are] precluded from earning their bread by the stoppage of trade, who must necessarily fall on people of condition for their maintenance." In a city that lived largely by trade, in a city that already had difficulty maintaining the poor, such considerations could not be dismissed lightly.[57]

Philadelphia's urban prominence also stood as an open invitation to invasion. It is not surprising, as Drowne observed, that "Some of the people in this City are apprehensive of several Ships of War, coming here." Costly defensive measures had to be taken. By the fall of 1775, a *chevaux-de-frise* of logs was sunk in the Delaware to keep the King's warships from the city. A number of galleys and floating batteries were also prepared to defend the city.[58]

Despite all optimistic assertions, no one dared claim that the dangers in opposing British rule were few. In June 1775, John Morton writing from Philadelphia said "we are really preparing for the worst that can happen, viz. a Civil War." The dangerous possibilities of such a war were amply demonstrated to Philadelphians in December of 1775. By the 5th of the month, the citizens were aware that Lord Dunmore, operating in Virginia, had issued a proclamation calling on blacks to fight for the King and in so doing to gain their freedom.[59] On December 14, Philadelphians learned that Dunmore's message had not gone unnoticed in the city. The *Evening Post* recounted the story of a "gentlewoman" who had supposedly been "insulted" by a black. When she "reprimanded" him, he said: "Stay, you d[amne]d white bitch, till Lord Dunmore and his black regiment come, and then we will see who is to take the wall." The black population of Philadelphia was rather small, so the threat of a local race war being part of a Civil War was not large. But in the colonies as a whole, about one in every five Americans was black. If great numbers of blacks joined the British, a military victory by the colonists would be difficult, perhaps impossible, to achieve.[60]

Such dangers merely added weight to the judgment of many Philadelphians that war was unwise. Certainly the Philadelphian who claimed that "Our politicks are all settled" was whistling in the dark. Those who opposed vigorous military action against England *did* find it dangerous to speak out. One such person, writing his sentiments to an Englishman in August 1775, pleaded "Conceal my name; or I should run a great risque of my life and property" for in Philadelphia "nobody dares to doubt" the American cause. But the threat of violence could only procure a partial silence: it could not change deeply held beliefs and many Philadelphians did oppose the war. In June 1775, a citizen observed that "If the [Continental] Congress were to hold up independence, the King might have by far the most friends here ... for all the best people are attached to him and the [British] constitution." Two months later, another Philadelphian proclaimed "I most heartily wish myself at home among freeborn Englishmen, not among this tyrannical and arbitrary rabble of America. ... If this [state of affairs in Philadelphia] be liberty, Good Lord deliver me from all such liberty!"[61]

There can be no question: many Philadelphians yearned for reconciliation with England. Indeed, it seems probable that most of the city's population wished for a cessation of hostilities. The Assembly of Pennsylvania reflected such a view when on November 9, 1775 it told the colony's delegates to the Continental Congress they were not to support or vote for any action that would lead to the independence of the colonies.[62] The problem was: could a mutually acceptable compromise between the English and American positions be found? Or were the differences so deep that a march toward an independent America was inevitable?[63] The events of 1776 would answer these questions. But the events of 1776 would also raise equally thorny questions for Philadelphia.

Philadelphians who opposed independence were dealt a severe blow on January 9, 1776, when Tom Paine's *Common Sense* was published in Philadelphia. Paine's essay was a masterpiece of emotion-laden political propaganda. He maintained that kings, especially English kings, did not rule by God's will or the will of the people. Rather, kings gained and held power by drenching the nation "in blood and ashes." The English form of government was not a glorious bulwark of freedom "because monarchy hath poisoned the Republic." A truly good government had to be fully republican, for "when Republican virtues fails [*sic*], slavery ensues." Now that America had "referred" the matter "from argument to arms," reconciliation with England was unwise and impossible. Independence was inevitable. And a declaration of independence would add powerful allies to America's already great military potential. America would win the war; her trade would flourish; she would become "the glory of the earth." And more. America would, in time, become "an asylum for mankind."[64] In a city that had been founded as a

"Holy Experiment" to achieve a virtuous and free society, this plea may well have struck a responsive note.[65]

The claim that reconciliation was impossible gained added weight on the very day *Common Sense* was published. The *Evening Post* on January 9 carried the full text of the King's speech of October 27, 1775. George III noted he had hoped Americans would come to their senses and turn their backs on those who supported war and independence. This had not happened and could not until British troops went to America. So the King was increasing his military power to crush the rebels. Only "submission" and "allegiance" to the English government would end hostilities.[66] Whether aided by the news of the King's action or not, Paine's pamphlet quickly became a colonial best seller. And John Adams asserted that its "clear, simple, concise" arguments on America's need and ability to attain independence were "generally approved."[67]

There is some question how "generally" Philadelphians accepted the idea of independence. But in January and February of 1776 the city's newspapers were virtually monopolized by writers who spoke in favor of independence. "Salus Populi," "Candidus," "Sincerus," "A Dialogue," "Questions and Answers" and "A Friend to Posterity and Mankind" argued that reconciliation with England was impossible, independence was the correct choice. If such was the case, it followed that the Assembly and those who opposed independence were shortsighted—or worse. "A Friend" shows the substance and tone of these arguments. He observed that while the "war sits heavy on us" he doubted that "all on a sudden [we shall] lose every desire of retaining our liberties." He felt "forced" to denounce "the artful, cunning and designing manner in which some men talk of reconciliation with Great-Britain, and the bug-bears they conjure up to frighten the timid, irresolute and ignorant, from a steady prosecution of those means, which alone can help us in our present circumstances." Those who favored reconciliation "love neither their country, nor their liberties, as much as something else."[68]

The call for throwing off the King was even offered in poem form. "R. R." observed:

> Some mice deep intrench'd in a rich Cheshire cheese,
>   Grimalkin long wish'd to devour,
> Secure, from their numbers, they liv'd at their ease,
>   And bravely defied his power.
>
> In vain all the day he sat watching their holes,
>   All his tricks and his force were in vain;

Each effort convinc'd him the vermin had souls,
Determined their cheese to maintain.
. . . .

"This cheese by possession we claim as our own,
"Fair freedon the claim doth approve;
"Our wants are but few, and her blessings alone,
"Sufficient those wants to remove.

"No cat will we own, with ambition run mad,
"For our KING——so move off in a trice;
"If we find, from exper'ence, a KING must be had,
"That KING shall be chose by the MICE."[69]

The arguments of those calling for independence were finally challenged in the public press on February 28. "Rationalis" maintained the time was not ripe for independence: reconciliation remained "the primary object of the dispute." He granted that the people of England seemed corrupt, yet held that when "properly balanced" the English form of government with a limited monarchy was as good a form of government as a free people could wish. A republican form of government, on the other hand, subverted liberty. In a republic, one party would gain dominance; then you had a "a many headed monster, a tyranny of many." Still, "Rationalis" conceded that if *future* events proved the need, he would then support a move for independence. Those who supported "Rationalis" could take heart for two reasons. The resolution of the Assembly against independence was still in effect and the press did say that British commissioners were to come to America "for conciliatory measures."[70]

Within five days of the appearance of "Rationalis' " essay, both the authority of the Assembly and possibility of commissioners achieving reconciliation came under sharp attack. On February 29, "The Apologist" offered a defense of the actions of the Assembly that was, in fact, an attack upon the Assembly. This essayist argued that the members of the legislature were not backward in their support of American liberty. Rather, they were honorable men who could not act more vigorously because, as honorable men, they could not violate the oaths of allegiance to the King they had to take to sit in the Assembly. What was needed was for the Committee of Inspection to call for a convention to handle the question of war and independence. Since the members of the convention would not have to take the oath, they could act more vigorously than the Assembly.[71] On March 4, the *Packet* reported that the Committee of Inspection did plan to call for a provincial convention to assess the state of affairs. As this potential challenge to the Assembly was mounted,

James Cannon, writing as "Cassandra," denounced the idea that British commissioners could bring reconciliation. The British were "arraying the greatest military force they can muster, and despatching them to butcher us with the utmost expedition." The suggestion that commissioners might bring reconciliation was an old ploy to "distract and divide the Colonies, by every hypocritical art in their power." Those Americans who supported the belief that commissioners could bring peace were only after "English Guineas . . . Pensions, and Titles in abundance."[72]

By early March, then, the exponents of independence had raised a massive verbal attack on the idea of avoiding independence by treating with British commissioners of peace. And they seemed ready to destroy the power of the Assembly to thwart the movement for independence. Unless the forces of moderation acted quickly, the push to independence might soon be unstoppable.

On March 9, Dr. William Smith, writing as "Cato," attempted to thwart those clamoring for independence. "Cato" affirmed that his pen would always work for what was "calculated to cement all parties in the Province, upon safe and popular grounds, . . . in executing the resolves of Congress, and maintaining *American* liberty." The best way to achieve this, "Cato" felt, was "promoting reconciliation upon constitutional principles between *Great Britain* and her Colonies." Having supported reconciliation, "Cato" turned to a defense of the Assembly. The Assembly was "vested with the authority of the people." Its "zeal" in defense of America was second to none among colonial governments. Indeed, the actions of the Assembly "have been the envy and admiration of our neighbours, who, enjoying no such perfection in their civil Constitutions, have been driven into the measure of Conventions." Should committees elected by a few be allowed to overthrow an Assembly "fairly and constitutionally elected"? "Would any wise people, enjoying such a Constitution, ever think of destroying it with their own hands?" The answers were so obvious, "Cato" did not bother to supply them.

In defending the Assembly, "Cato" became almost as venomous as "Cassandra." "Ambition" needed "to be checked in the lowest as the highest." Those who wanted to "Succeed in assuming the power of Government" by a convention were "a few men, who consider themselves as leaders in the city of *Philadelphia.*"[73]

On the day that "Cato's" essay appeared, Philadelphians learned that a provincial conference, which might undermine the power of the Assembly, would not be held. On the 9th, the *Evening Post* carried an item dated

March 5. The Committee of Inspection for the City and Liberties on that date sent a letter to the county committees of Pennsylvania. That letter noted that the city committee had planned to call a provincial conference. Such a meeting seemed necessary because the three eastern counties were unfairly overrepresented in the Assembly and the members of the three eastern counties formed "the opposition given to the present measures" needed to defend America. The committee noted, "As the present unequal representation is the ground of every other complaint, the Committee had this *principally* in view. There are others which are attended with immediate danger." Among those "other" complaints was listed "the instructions given to them [delegates to Congress], by which they are bound to disclose every, even military, movement; and are prevented from the free exercise of their judgments as the necessity of the times may require appear unsafe, as well as dishonorable; to have a direct tendency to countenance the illiberal insinuations of our enemies; . . . and to mislead the neighbouring Colonies into a false opinion of the sense of this province."

The call for a convention to deal with such problems was canceled because of a meeting between the Philadelphia Committee of Inspection and "several" members of the Assembly. Those Assemblymen convinced the committee that a more equal representation would be forthcoming "and that the other matters would be attended to." It is essential to understand the position of the Philadelphia committee. The committee demanded not simply a more equal Assembly; it also demanded reconsideration of the November 9, 1775 Assembly resolution, which said that the delegates to the Continental Congress could not vote for independence. The Philadelphia committee wanted a more equal representation; they also wanted, with or without that equal representation, the right to have Pennsylvania vote for independence.[74]

The meeting between the Philadelphia Committee of Inspection and members of the Assembly bore fruit. On March 23, the Assembly voted to add seventeen new members to its number. The city of Philadelphia would gain four new representatives; western counties would gain thirteen additional representatives. An election to select these additional representatives was to be held on May 1.[75] Complaints by Philadelphia and the west that they were underrepresented in the Assembly had often been voiced before.[76] Why had the Assembly finally listened in March 1776? An essayist who supported independence and giving the vote to every man who was for America's "liberty" saw sinister motives. He saw persons supporting a more equal representation engaged in a "manoeuvre" that "would have a tendency to quiet the people, by taking one of the most unanswerable objections to the present Administration out of their mouths. You cannot, however, forget that this partial redress was a very late one, and only conceded to prevent a radical reformation."[77]

It is not clear if the expansion of the Assembly was a "manoeuvre" to short-circuit the drive for independence and restructuring of the local government.[78] But the action of the legislature did focus Philadelphia's political attention on May 1 when the four additional Assemblymen would be elected. In March and April, persons strongly for and against independence and a new form of local government battled to attract the city's electorate. In these months, Philadelphians were subjected to a veritable barrage of political essays.

Led by the writings of "Cato," the "moderates" presented two basic arguments. Independence, with its frightening horror of prolonged war, was not inevitable. Peace on terms that would protect America's liberties was yet possible. Indeed, only fools and demagogues would turn their backs on the possibility of reconciliation on honorable terms. Equally important, Pennsylvania's legally constituted Assembly government was a shining example of equal and free government. Pennsylvania had and would continue to prosper under this fair government. To destroy it would be the height of stupidity.[79]

The "radicals" also presented two basic arguments. The calls for reconciliation with England were an open invitation to disaster. The commissioners only had authority to pardon those who acknowledged England's total power over the colonies. Nothing less than independence would protect American liberty and allow her to stand as an example of freedom to all mankind. It followed that one must vote for persons who would support independence. And one must also vote to change the government of Pennsylvania. The Assembly had not only been against independence; it had been against equality. Pennsylvania's government was a government for the few, especially the rich few. This last point the radicals hammered hard. Voting restrictions based on economic power should be cast aside so that all men who supported independence could vote. The rich who yearned for reconciliation to continue their monopoly of power had to be dethroned.[80]

The radicals had good reason to hope that appeals to economic concerns would touch a nerve with Philadelphians. From January to May 1776, the purchasing power of Continental currency was slowly losing ground to hard money. And those in the employ of the American cause were paid in Continental currency.[81] In late February, the Philadelphia Associators had evidenced concern over their economic position. They noted their number was made up chiefly of tradesmen and others, "who earn their living by their industry." Constant employment was a necessity. To insure that they had jobs, the Associators requested that only persons from their ranks be employed to perform publicly supported jobs. And such work should be "equally" divided among them "as conveniently" as possible.[82] In early March, the city's Committee of Inspection observed that the price of many items, including salt, rum, sugar, spice, molasses, coco and coffee, was being "artificial[ly]" raised. This was "at any time shameful, but at a period of public calamity most barbarous and oppressive, more especially on the poor and the middling ranks of life." To stop this evil, the committee published a price list for such items and decreed that anyone who demanded more than the published price would be punished.[83] "An Enemy to Monopolizing," noting that the Assembly had not stopped price gouging, asserted that those who drove up prices for personal gain "endeavor to oppress and destroy the poor, and by this means destroy our noble opposition to tyranny and arbitrary taxation." Indeed, monopolizers were quite likely in the British pay.[84] If the radicals by using such arguments could lay the city's economic difficulties at the feet of those who supported reconciliation, many votes might be won for independence.

When reading the extensive public debate on independence and the nature of Pennsylvania's government, it is easy to lose sight of two critical facts. There was, in Philadelphia, a core of activists against independence. That is clear. But this fact tells us little about what the mass of Philadelphians felt. And we must try to understand what the so-called "inarticulate" citizens felt if we are to understand the Philadelphia of 1776.[85] A second vital fact that must be kept in mind is that the essays published by the moderates pleaded for reconciliation "*if it has for its basis an effectual security for the liberties of America.*" Even the moderates supported resistance to the supposed British tyranny. They publicly accepted the need for independence *if* future events proved a reconciliation on reasonable American terms an impossibility.[86]

Most analysts have argued that the results of the May 1 election show that Philadelphia "hung in a delicate balance" between independence and the hope for reconciliation. The moderate candidates received the following votes: Samuel Howell, 941; Andrew Allen, 923; Alexander Wilcox, 921; Thomas Willing, 911. The candidates for independence received: George Clymer, 923; Mark Kuhl, 904; Owen Biddle, 903; Daniel Roberdeau, 890. The moderates thus won three assembly seats and the independents only one. But as one historian noted, a switch of only eleven votes would have reversed the results. Nevertheless, on May 1 the majority of Philadelphians rejected the call for independence. Or did they?[87]

There is good reason to question the claim that the May 1 vote accurately reflected the view of the majority of Philadelphians. By law, the franchise was limited to those who owned a freehold of fifty acres or who were worth £50 clear estate. If such restrictions were strictly enforced, less than 400, or only about one in fifty, Philadelphians could have voted on May 1.[88] But the number of votes cast on that day—1,850 to 1,860—indicates that the franchise requirements were not strictly enforced or that they could be circumvented. The key to the large vote seems to be the election law, which allowed a person to take an oath, given by an inspector of elections, which said he possessed the necessary property qualifications.

Does this mean any adult male could vote? Hardly. If a person was convicted of falsely swearing he had the necessary property to vote he would: (1) have his vote thrown out, (2) be subject to a £5 fine, and (3) be subject to the criminal penalty for perjury. Obviously it made a great difference who was an inspector of elections. An inspector who felt you would vote the way he wanted might not challenge you even if you were clearly lying about your economic worth. Still, inspectors ran a risk if they played too fast and loose with the voting requirements. An election official "legally convicted" of "willful fraud" was to be fined £100 and to "be forever thereafter disabled from holding . . . any office of honor, trust or profit" in Pennsylvania."[89] These facts suggest that while the Philadelphia franchise on May 1 was not restricted to the economic elite, the poorer Philadelphians were the citizens most likely to have been unable to vote. In the Philadelphia of May 1776, elections were obviously a highly complicated matter.

It must also be remembered that the election of May 1 was for four Assemblymen to represent the city of Philadelphia. And as *legally* defined, Philadelphia ended at Vine and South Streets. It appears that the May 1 election was limited to those who lived in the legally defined city.[90] Thus the Philadelphians of Southwark and the Northern Liberties did not vote in the May 1 election. And as a group, the citizens of those areas were members of Philadelphia's less prosperous groups.[91]

To the extent that the election of May 1 excluded Philadelphians, it excluded the poorer Philadelphians. The question is: were the less prosperous Philadelphians more likely to support independence. Alexander Graydon thought so. He felt that "opposition to the claims of Britain originated with the better sort." But in 1776, "as whigism declined among the higher classes, it increased in the inferior." Graydon's assertions are supported by the views of other contemporaries.[92] Thus it appears that the "inferior" classes were likely to support the move for independence. And it was the "inferior" Philadelphians who were most likely to be unable to vote on May 1. Considering all this, it seems logical to conclude that despite the seeming "delicate balance" of May 1, the majority of Philadelphians were for independence.

If in fact Philadelphia did hang in a "delicate balance" between independence and reconciliation, that balance was soon tipped. A postscript to the *Packet,* dated May 6, carried the news that 20,000 foreign troops had been hired by Britain. And there was to be in April "a large naval force . . . coming out for America" carrying 45,000 troops to squash the American rebellion. The *Packet* asked: *"Oh GEORGE! Are these thy commissioners of peace and reconciliation?"* On May 8, the city was thrown into "confusion" as *H.M.S. Roebuck,* with forty-four guns, and *H.M.S. Liverpool,* with twenty-eight guns, sailed to attack the city. The colonial gondolas gave battle for four hours. The next day, as "many thousand spectators" watched, the fight was renewed until the British ships withdrew. The shooting war had finally come to Philadelphia.[93]

"Cato" and the other moderates were now apparently trapped by events. Knowing that thousands of enemy troops were coming, any talk of reconciliation must have seemed out of place amid the smell of gunpowder and the flash of cannon. In a perverse way, George III, *H.M.S. Roebuck* and *H.M.S. Liverpool* seemed to be casting votes for independence.

The move to independence was given a great push by the Continental Congress on May 10 when John Adams proposed, and the Congress adopted, a resolution that "where no government sufficient to the exigencies of . . . affairs" had been adopted, such governments should be established. That seems innocent enough. But this resolution was packed with independent dynamite, as the preamble to the resolution, adopted on May 15, revealed. That preamble asserted that oaths and affirmations for support of the King were "absolutely irreconcilable to reason and good conscience." Thus, "it is necessary that the exercise of every kind of authority under the said crown should be totally suppressed." In Pennsylvania, Assemblymen still took the oath of allegiance to George III. The very government of the colony rested on a grant given by an English monarch. Thus, no less a body than the Continental Congress appeared to sanction the overthrow of the Pennsylvania government and a call for independence. In fact, Adams argued that the resolution was, "on all hands, considered by men of understanding as equivalent to a declaration of independence."[94]

The events of early May brought decisive measures. Dr. James Clitherall, who was in the city, argued while "parties ran high" in Philadelphia "—the body of the people were for Independency." On May 20, "notwithstanding the rain," an estimated 4,000 people met in the State House yard. The meeting passed resolves proclaiming the Assembly unworthy of confidence, especially given its unrescinded directive of November 9, 1775 against a vote for independence. The meeting further resolved that the present government was incompetent to produce a new constitution and so a provincial convention for that purpose should be called. According to Christopher Marshall, there was but one dissenting vote to these resolutions. But if Dr. Clitherall was correct, dissent was virtually impossible. He claimed "the people behaved in such a tyran[n]ical manner that the least opposition was dangerous. ... I therefore thought it prudent to vote with the multitude."[95]

The moderates worked hard to promote a petition rejecting the ideas of the May 20 meeting. A reported 6,000 persons in Pennsylvania signed this petition by May 29. Numerous groups, including the Philadelphia County Committee of Inspection, sided with the moderates. On June 7, the moderates' position was weakened when Richard Henry Lee of Virginia proposed to the Continental Congress that the colonies should declare their independence. The next day, the Pennsylvania Assembly rescinded its resolution of November 9. Pennsylvania's delegates could now vote for independence if they felt it was necessary.[96] On June 18, a Provincial Conference elected by Pennsylvania's Committees of Inspection met in Philadelphia. This meeting argued that a Provincial Convention must be convened to draw up a new form of government for the colony. July 8 was set as the day for the election of delegates to this convention. The conference also said it would support a declaration of independence if that was Congress's wish. In calling on the colony for 4,500 troops to repel an expected British attack on New York, the conference showed it felt independence was inevitable. The plea was made: "It is now in your power to immortalize your names, by mingling your achievements with the events of the year 1776–a year which we hope will be famed in the annals of history to the end of time, for establishing upon a lasting foundation the liberties of one-quarter of the globe."[97] June was a bad month for the moderates. July would be a disaster.

On Tuesday, July 2, the Continental Congress declared the "United Colonies ... Free and Independent States." Four days later the *Evening Post* became the first newspaper in the land to publish the text of the Declaration of Independence.[98] On the 8th, amid "warm sunshine," John Nixon read the Declaration in the State House yard. Charles Biddle, who was there, asserted that "very few respectable people" were present. Deborah Logan agreed. She observed that "the first audience of the Declaration was neither very numerous nor composed of the *most respectable* class of citizens." It appears that the wealthy moderates as well as the Tories stayed home. Those persons who did hear Nixon "declared their approbation by three repeated huzzas." Soon thereafter, the King's Arms were removed from the Supreme Court room in the State House. Around five o'clock, the Declaration was read to each of the five battalions of Associators drawn up on the commons. In the "fine starlight, pleasant evening," bonfires were lit. The King's Arms provided fuel for one of them. Bells rang throughout the city. All in all, the celebration was orderly and rather subdued.[99]

On the day that Philadelphians celebrated the Declaration of Independence, they also had the opportunity to vote for members of the Constitutional Convention. This was not mere chance. The Philadelphia Committe of Inspection united the celebration and the vote in an apparent attempt to influence voters to select only firm patriots.[100] Considering the rules of that election, it hardly seemed necessary. For this election, the franchise was extended to all Associators, age twenty-one, who had resided in the state for one year and who had paid or been rated for provincial or county taxes. However, the vote would be denied to any person a committee of inspection had branded as an enemy to America unless that person had been "restored to favor." Further, persons qualified to vote for Assemblymen under the old restrictive property requirements could be required to swear they: (1) held no allegiance to the King or England; (2) did not oppose the convention's right to establish a "free" government for Pennsylvania; and (3) supported the measures adopted by the Continental Congress in opposition to British "tyranny." Finally, before anyone could sit in the convention, he had to swear a similar oath, which included the promise "to establish and support a government in this province on the authority of the people only." In short, those who favored independence and a new form of government stacked the deck.[101]

There are no recorded returns for the Philadelphia election of July 8. But it appears the turnout was light and that tories and moderates stayed away in droves. Certainly the Constitutional Convention, which met in Philadelphia from July 15 to September 28, was dominated by radicals.[102] And the frame of government they produced was truly revolutionary. Under this new constitution, the vote was given to all adult freemen who had lived in the state for one year and paid public taxes. The governor was replaced by a Supreme Executive Council of twelve members. There was no veto power. A unicameral legislature held virtually all political power. It could remove any official, including judges, deemed guilty of "mal-administration." Judges of the Supreme Court were to be appointed by the legislature and could be removed "at any time" for "misbehavior." This constitution was not submitted to the citizens for a vote of ratification. It was merely proclaimed by the convention as the organic law on September 28.[103]

The creation of a new government for the state threw the government of the legally defined city of Philadelphia into confusion. Until 1776, the city had been run by a closed and self-perpetuating corporation that held power under a charter granted by William Penn. With the change in government, that charter "became void." The mayor, recorder and aldermen of the city ceased to function. But the laws authorizing aid to the city's poor, the lighting and cleaning of streets and other needed urban tasks could not function properly without these officials. Nothing was done about this problem in 1776. So as the year ended, the government of Philadelphia rested in uncertainty. The old government was dead but nothing had yet been established to take its place.[104]

In the last half of the year, the disarray and problems of governing the city were matched by economic difficulty. In July the paper currency used to pay publicly employed persons would buy 8 percent less than hard money. By September it would buy 14 percent less, and in November 25 percent less. As the purchasing power of the Continental dollar declined, prices rose "briskly" in the last nine months of the year. From November to December, the median price of wholesale goods rose a staggering 25 percent. The Committee of Inspection could do little to stop these price increases. From early June until the committee was dissolved on September 17, the committee was only empowered to regulate the price of salt and tea.[105]

The rise in prices and the press of war proved that earlier fears that additional numbers of poor would have to be supported were well founded. In July large numbers of militia were called into active service. "Many" of these men "left families who are destitute of the means of acquiring an honest living." These "poor families" had to be maintained. And so in August money was collected and given to them by the local committees.[106] Thus, the cost of poor relief was increasing; the economy was racked by inflationary prices and a depreciating paper currency. By late 1776, Philadelphia's economic state was, at best, precarious.

The military situation was just as bleak. In early November, rumors began to circulate that General Howe planned to attack Philadelphia. On the 15th, handbills were published asking Pennsylvanians "to put themselves in a martial array" and to be ready to march to Philadelphia's defense "with the utmost expedition." By December 2, the city was "alarmed" by the news that Howe's army was at Brunswick and "proceeding for this place." Fear gripped many. Wagons were loaded with belongings; numbers fled the city. Martial law was declared on the 8th. The next day, all shops were ordered closed and the militia marched "into the Jesseys" to attack Howe. "Confusion" reigned, and not just among the citizens. On December 11, the Continental Congress fled to Baltimore. After Congress left Philadelphia, it was hinted that the Continental army would burn the city rather than let it fall to the British. Israel Putnam, the general in charge of defending Philadelphia, issued a public denial on December 13. He assured the citizens that Congress and General Washington had ordered him to "consider every attempt to burn the city of Philadelphia as a crime of the blackest dye." Anyone trying to fire the city would "without ceremony" be "punish[ed] capitally." A day later, Putnam added "the Congress have ordered the City to be defended to the last extremity."[107]

The last extremity was not necessary in 1776. The dramatic crossing of the Delaware on Christmas Eve and the subsequent American victory at the battles of Trenton and Princeton canceled Howe's immediate plans to "pay a visit" to Philadelphia. But the city could not rest easy. Howe might yet come. The city might yet be destroyed.[108] As 1777 dawned, Philadelphians were in a tortuous limbo. Nothing seemed certain save that the near future was sure to be dramatic and dangerous. Yet Philadelphians, as persons must, faced the future with as much certainty as they could muster. And for different Philadelphians of different philosophical persuasions, there existed a strange mix of hopes and fears.

WHITHER INDEPENDENCE

In 1776 Philadelphians had to decide two fundamental questions: Would they support independence? Would they change the basic structure of local government? The debate over independence was sharp, heated. Yet the great majority of Philadelphians quickly reconciled themselves to independence once it was proclaimed. The great majority of moderates who said they would support independence if, in time, it seemed necessary to defend America did just that.[109] The change in Philadelphia's city government occurred as a direct result of independence. In 1776 there was no great debate on the merits of keeping the old government. It died quietly, almost unnoticed and, at the time, little lamented.[110] The decision to alter the state's government was another story. Many refused to accept it and worked for years to destroy it.

It was easy and, most would say, reasonable to dislike much about the Constitution of 1776. The Executive Council of Twelve could not provide the clear, vigorous leadership that a governor could. The document *did* threaten the existence of an independent judiciary by saying that appointed judges could be removed for the vaguely termed evil of "misbehavior." The Constitution of 1776, often held up as an example of democratic thought, was not submitted to the people for ratification. If that is democracy, it is a strange variety.[111]

The evils that many saw in the new government were tied to the fact that virtually all power rested in the hands of a unicameral legislature. Because this was true, the franchise requirement was judged of critical importance. The debate over the franchise tells us a good deal about what Philadelphia had been and might become.

"Peter Easy" spoke for those who supported the long-established view that voters should have a material stake in society. The vote had to be kept from "people without property ... [for] such people, having nothing to lose, and a prospect of gaining by public convulsions, are always the most ready to engage in seditious, tumult[u]ous and factious proceedings." They were easy prey for "ambitious, daring, wicked men." "Easy" asserted that limiting the vote to those worth £50 created no hardship. "A large majority" of freemen were worth £50. Indeed, persons not worth that amount could be dismissed as "indolent or prodigal." He spoke from the heart as well as the mind when he plaintively asked: "Cant the liberties and happiness of *Pennsylvania* be trusted to those men in it, who are worth *fifty* pounds each?"

"Peter Easy's" comments were offered as part of "A Dialogue" with an "Orator." The "Orator" rejected "Easy's" claims. Fifty pounds was not easy to obtain: under the old franchise law not one in five adult male Associators were qualified to vote. (At least for Philadelphia, "Orator" was here on firm ground.) In his eyes, the Constitution of 1776 was a noble document precisely because it gave *"every freeman"* the vote. Indeed, "now *all men* will be put on a level with respect to THIS GRAND RIGHT OF VOTING AT ELECTIONS, and that may in time bring them to a level *in every other respect,* as has happened in other countries."[112]

This "Dialogue" illustrates the clash between two casts of mind that did battle in 1776. "Easy" looked to a past where political power rested with the owners of substantial property. He feared the masses. "Orator" had faith in the masses. He wanted an egalitarian society where power would rest with people simply because they were people. "Orator" was an ardent democrat. As this debate shows, what was at stake in the Philadelphia of 1776 was the very nature of society. "Orator" had dreams; "Easy" had nightmares.

In the Philadelphia of 1776, there was no guarantee that independence would be achieved. Saying you are independent and winning a war of independence are two quite different things. Nor was it clear if the Constitution of 1776 would endure and be a great engine for social change. Only time would tell and even a century later the answers might not be entirely clear.[113]

NOTES

1. Philadelphia was less than a century old in 1776. Southwark and the Northern Liberties, while not legally a part of Philadelphia in 1776, were integral parts of the city (see note 29). As used in this study, unless otherwise noted, the term Philadelphia or its equivalent includes Southwark and the Northern Liberties.
2. Samuel Hazard, ed., *Register of Pennsylvania . . .,* 16 vols. (Philadelphia: Hazard, 1828–36), 2:346; 3:40; John F. Watson, *Annals of Philadelphia . . . ,* enlarged by Willias P. Hazard, 3 vols. (Philadelphia: Edwin S. Stuart, 1905), 1:103, 231, 406–07; 2:420–21 (hereafter cited as Watson, *Annals*).
3. See, e.g., Frederick Law Olmsted, Jr. and Theodora Kimball, eds., *Frederick Law Olmsted: Landscape Architect 1822–1903,* 2 vols. (New York: G. P. Putnam's Sons, 1922–28), 2:161–65, 188, 192–95; Ernest S. Griffith, *A History of American City Government [:] The Conspicuous Failure, 1870–1900* (New York: Praeger, 1974), p. 175.
4. Andrew Burnaby, *Travels Through the Middle Settlements in North-America* [1759–1760], 2d ed. (London: T. Payne, 1775), p. 55 and Newton D. Mereness, ed., *Travels in the American Colonies* (New York: Macmillan, 1916), p. 411.
5. "Amnicolist" is typical of the classical pseudonyms used by eighteen-century correspondents. *The Pennsylvania Packet and the General Advertiser,* February 10, 1772 (hereafter cited as *Penn Packet*) and Rush to Noah Webster, February 13, 1788, in *Letters of Benjamin Rush,* ed. by L. H. Butterfield, 2 vols. (Princeton: Princeton University Press, 1951), 1:450.
6. P. 10 and Alexander Graydon, *Memoirs of a Life . . .* (Harrisburg: John Wyeth, 1811), p. 37.
7. John K. Alexander, "The Philadelphia Numbers Game: An Analysis of Philadelphia's Eighteenth-Century Population," *The Pennsylvania Magazine of History and Biography,* 98 (July 1974) :314–24, especially 324 (hereafter cited as *PMHB*) and Carl Bridenbaugh, *Cities in Revolt: Urban Life in America, 1743–1776,* rev. ed. (New York: Oxford University Press, 1971) pp. 5, 216.
8. Quotations from Arthur L. Jensen, *The Maritime Commerce of Colonial Philadelphia* (Ann Arbor: Edwards Brothers, 1963), p. 5 and see also pp. 5–9 passim.
9. Ibid., pp. 8–9; Bridenbaugh, *Cities in Revolt,* pp. 75, 268–69; Carl Bridenbaugh and Jessica Bridenbaugh, *Rebels and Gentlemen: Philadelphia in the Age of Franklin* (New York: Reynal & Hitchcock, 1942), p. 10; Burnaby, *Travels,* p. 58.
10. Nicholas Cresswell, *The Journal of Nicholas Cresswell 1774–1777,* Samuel Thornbely, ed. (New York: Dial, 1924), p. 156 (hereafter cited as Cresswell, *Journal*); see also Solomon Drowne, "Dr. Solomon Drowne," Harrold E. Gillingham, ed.,

in *PMHB* 48:3 (1924) : 239 (hereafter cited as Drowne); Patrick M'Robert, *A Tour Through Part of the North Provinces of America . . . in the Years 1774 & 1775*, Carl Bridenbaugh, ed. (New York: Arno Press, 1968 [originally published in *PMHB* 59 (April 1935) : 134–180]), p. 31 (hereafter cited as M'Robert, *Tour*); Robert Honyman, *Colonial Panorama 1775: Dr. Robert Honyman's Journal for March and April*, Philip Padelford, ed. (San Marino: The Huntington Library, 1939), p. 14 (hereafter cited as Honyman, *Journal*); Bridenbaugh, *Cities in Revolt*, pp. 72, 269.

11. List drawn from Hannah B. Roach, "Taxables in the City of Philadelphia, 1756," *The Pennsylvania Genealogical Magazine* 21:1 (1961), 10–24 passim. For a similar list of 1774, see Sam Bass Warner, Jr., *The Private City: Philadelphia in Three Periods of Its Growth* (Philadelphia: University of Pennsylvania Press, 1968), p. 18.

12. Quotation from Carroll Frey, *The Independence Square Neighborhood* (Philadelphia: The Beck Engraving Company, 1926), p. 19 and see also the map that accompanies *Historic Philadelphia* (American Philosophical Society, *Transactions*, New Ser., 43 [1953], Part 1); John W. Reps, *The Making of Urban America . . .* (Princeton: Princeton University Press, 1965), pp. 168, 171; M'Robert, *Tour*, p. 29; Jacob Duche, *Caspipina's Letters . . .*, 2 vols. (2d ed.; Bath, England: R. Cruttwell, 1777), 1:8.

13. Serle to Earl of Dartmouth, January 10, 1778 in Benjamin Stevens, ed., *B. F. Steven's Facsimilies . . .*, 24 vols. (London: Malby & Sons, 1889–95), no. 2075; cf. Drowne, p. 238 and Honyman, *Journal*, p. 19.

14. M'Robert, *Tour*, p. 30; *The North-American and the West-Indian Gazatteer* (London: G. Robinson, 1776), under "Phila"; Watson, *Annals*, 1:221; Frey, *Independence Square Neighborhood*, p. 13; James Mease, *The Picture of Philadelphia . . .* (Philadelphia: B. & T. Kite, 1811), p. 25.

15. Drowne, p. 236; Honyman, *Journal*, pp. 16–17; M'Robert, *Tour*, p. 30.

16. Drowne, p. 239; see also Cresswell, *Journal*, p. 155 and Honyman, *Journal*, p. 15.

17. Quotations from Honyman, *Journal*, pp. 15, 18; see also Drowne, p. 238; Watson, *Annals*, 1:383; 3:206; M'Robert, *Tour*, pp. 30–31; Burnaby, *Travels*, pp. 54–55; *Historic Philadelphia*, passim; but for a slightly different view, see Cresswell, *Journal*, p. 155.

18. Richard Gimbel, *Thomas Paine: A Bibliographical Check List of COMMON SENSE . . .* (New Haven: Yale University Press, 1956), p. 16. *The Pennsylvania Magazine: or, American Monthly Museum*, which was first published in January 1775, ceased publication in July 1776.

19. Drowne, p. 237.

20. M'Robert, *Tour*, p. 29; John Adams, *Diary and Autobiography of John Adams*, L. H. Butterfield, ed., 4 vols. (Cambridge: Harvard University Press, 1961), 2:157, for Adams' negative comments see, e.g., Ibid., p. 150; Cresswell, *Journal*, p. 156 and cf. p. 155.

21. Writing in 1794, Henry Wansey observed "the noise of the croaking frogs, and tree toads, was intolerable, for they abound in the environs of this city." I am assuming that frogs and toads had the same bad habits in 1776. See his *Journal of an Excursion to the United States of North America* (Salisbury, England: J. Easton, 1796), p. 185.

22. *Journal*, p. 20 and cf. Bridenbaugh, *Cities in Revolt*, pp. 33–34, 238–39, 241.

23. Bridenbaugh, *Cities in Revolt*, pp. 106, 109, 296, 297.

24. *The Pennsylvania Gazette*, April 11, 1765 (hereafter cited as *Penn. Gazette*) and broadside "By the Mayor, Recorder, and Aldermen, and the Commissioners for paving and cleansing the Streets, &c." (Philadelphia: B. Franklin and D. Hall, 1765).

25. *The Pennsylvania Chronical and Universal Advertiser*, March 20–27, 1769.

26. Rush to John Swanick, n.d., which appeared in *The Independent Gazetteer*, December 21, 1793; see also Graydon, *Memoirs*, p. 34.
27. Watson, *Annals*, 1:101; 2:411. Bridenbaugh (*Cities in Revolt*, pp. 74, 240–41) holds that while the city was filthy to the early 1760's, it was rather clean by the 1770's.
28. John C. Lowber, ed., *Ordinances of the Corporation of the City of Philadelphia . . .* (Philadelphia: Moses Thomas, 1812), pp. 1–10; J. Thomas Scharf and Thompson Westcott, *History of Philadelphia. 1609–1884*, 3 vols. (Philadelphia: L. H. Everts, 1884), 1:174–75 and map between pp. 96 and 97; John Daly and Allen Weinberg, *Genealogy of Philadelphia County Subdivisions*, 2d ed. (Philadelphia: Department of Records, 1966), pp. 1–3, 10, 54, 56, 57.
29. Warner, *Private City*, pp. 11–14; James T. Mitchell and Henry Flanders, comps., *The Statutes at Large of Pennsylvania from 1682 to 1801*, 15 vols. (Harrisburg: various State Printers, 1896–1911), 6:214–22; 14:31–38 and cf. wording of these laws to Ibid., 6:200 (hereafter cited as *Penn. Statutes*).
30. Gertrude MacKinney and Charles F. Hoban, eds., *Pennsylvania Archives: Eighth Series* [Votes and Proceedings of the House of Representatives of the Province of Pennsylvania, 1682–1776], 8 vols. (N.p.: n.p., 1931–35), 7:5506, 6148 (hereafter cited as *Penn. Arch.*, 8th ser.).
31. Ibid., 7:5823–24, 5829, 5830–31, 5857, 6148.
32. *Penn. Statutes*, 7:9–17 passim.
33. Quotations from *Penn. Arch.*, 8th ser., 7:6098, 6099 and see also pp. 6097, 6101, 6322–24, 6337, 6343, 6369.
34. "W. R.," *Penn. Gazette*, January 9, 1772.
35. *Minutes of the Managers of the House of Employment*, May 20, 1769 to August 11, 1778, pp. 226–233 with quotation at p. 226 deposited in The Archives of the City and County of Philadelphia in record group 35.3.
36. Duke De La Fochefoucault Liancourt, *Travels Through The United States of North America . . .*, 2 vols. (London: T. Davison, 1799), 2:382 and see also petition of vendue masters of Southwark and the Northern Liberties of c. 1791, deposited at the Historical Society of Pennsylvania in the Society Miscellaneous Collection (hereafter cited as HSP).
37. Report of Managers of House of Employment: Comittee on Condition of the House, February 9, 1768, deposited at HSP in Edward Wanton Smith Collection.
38. *Penn. Packet*, October 26, 1772 and see also John K. Alexander, "Philadelphia's 'Other Half': Attitudes Toward Poverty and the Meaning of Poverty in Philadelphia, 1760–1800" (Ph. D. dissertation, University of Chicago, 1973), pp. 45–50.
39. Watson, *Annals*, 1:176, 186–91 passim, whose views on the clothing of the lower classes is supported by Ian M. G. Quimby, "Apprenticeship in Colonial Philadelphia" (M. A. thesis, University of Delaware, 1962), p. 62. See also "Queries," *Penn. Packet*, March 18, 1776 and "Effects," *Penn. Gazette*, February 12, 1767.
40. *The Pennsylvania Journal, and Weekly Advertiser*, May 15, 1760 (hereafter cited as *Penn. Journal*).
41. *Penn. Packet*, January 1, 1776.
42. Ibid., November 9, 1772.
43. January 19, 1774.
44. This remained true well after 1776. See, e.g., Charles Peale in *The New World*, January 6, 1797; "Philanthropos," *The True American and Commercial Advertiser*, November 6, 1798; *The Philadelphia Minerva*, April 11, 1795.
45. Warner, *Private City*, p. 9 and see corresponding note 14.
46. Richard M. Brown, "Violence and the American Revolution," in Stephen G. Kurtz and James H. Hutson, eds., *Essays on the American Revolution* (Chapel Hill: University of North Carolina Press, 1973), pp. 81–120 and especially pp. 97, 119–20.

47. Margaret W. Willard, ed., *Letters on the American Revolution 1774–1776* (Boston: Houghton Mifflin, 1925), pp. 37–38.
48. Scharf and Westcott, *History,* 1:289ff.
49. Honyman, *Journal,* p. 29.
50. Christopher Marshall, *Extracts from the Diary of Christopher Marshall, Kept in Philadelphia and Lancaster . . . 1774–1781,* William Duane, ed. (Albany: Joel Munsell, 1877), pp. 17, 18 (hereafter cited as Marshall, *Diary*) and Scharf and Westcott, *History,* 1:295.
51. Drowne, p. 242.
52. Samuel Curwen, *The Journal of Samuel Curwen: Loyalist,* Andrew Oliver, ed., 2 vols. (Cambridge: Harvard University Press, 1972), 1:4.
53. Willard, ed., *Letters,* pp. 101, 103. These were clearly exaggerated claims. See, e.g., Ibid., 162.
54. Quoted in Theodore Thayer, *Pennsylvania Politics and the Growth of Democracy 1740–1776* (Harrisburg: Pennsylvania Historical and Museum Commission, 1953), p. 106.
55. Marshall, *Diary,* p. 23; Samuel Curwen, *Journal and Letters . . .,* George A. Ward, ed. (New York: C. S. Francis, 1842), p. 29.
56. Willard, ed., *Letters,* pp. 72, 94, 162–63.
57. Ibid., pp. 103, 162, 213 and Edmund C. Burnett, ed., *Letters of the Members of the Continental Congress,* 8 vols. (Washington, D.C.: Carnegie Institution, 1921–38), 1:114.
58. Drowne, p. 242; Scharf and Westcott, *History,* 1:299ff.; Willard, ed., *Letters,* p. 211.
59. Burnett, ed., *Letters,* 1:114, 270.
60. Gary B. Nash, "Slaves and Slaveowners in Colonial Philadelphia," *William and Mary Quarterly,* 3d ser., 30 (April 1973) : 237 and Evarts B. Greene and Virginia D. Harrington, *American Population Before the Federal Census of 1790* (New York: Columbia University Press, 1932), pp. 6–8.
61. Willard, ed., *Letters,* pp. 123, 179–80, 182, 183 and see sources in the following note.
62. Resolution is in *Penn. Statutes,* 8:493–94 and on general feelings see Wallace Brown, *The King's Friends: The Composition and Motives of the American Loyalist Claimants* (Providence: Brown University Press, 1965), pp. 130–31.
63. For a cogent analysis of the problems see Charles M. Andrews, *The Colonial Background of the American Revolution,* rev. ed. (New Haven: Yale University Press, 1931), especially pp. 173–220.
64. Thomas Paine, *The Writings of Thomas Paine,* Moncure D. Conway, comp. and ed., 4 vols. (New York: G. P. Putnam's Sons, 1894), 1:69–120 with quotation from pp. 83, 85, 93, 101.
65. Scharf and Westcott, *History,* 1:79, 90–91, 113–15.
66. *The Pennsylvania Evening Post* (hereafter cited as *Penn. Eve. Post*).
67. Gimbel, *Thomas Paine,* pp. 49, 57 and John Adams, *The Works of John Adams,* Charles F. Adams, ed., 10 vols. (Boston: Little, Brown, 1850–56), 1:205.
68. In the order listed in the text, these essays appeared in *Penn. Journal,* February 2, 1776; *Penn. Eve. Post,* February 3 and 13, 1776; *Penn. Packet,* February 19, 1776; *Penn. Eve. Post,* February 17, 1776; *Penn. Packet,* February 12, 1776. See also "Salus Populi," *Penn. Journal,* December 12, 1775 where the author suggested that independence might well be essential.
69. *Penn. Eve. Post,* February 17, 1776.
70. This essay appeared in *Penn. Gazette.* A poem with one line attacking the author of *Common Sense* but with no arguments on Paine's points appeared in *Penn. Eve. Post,* February 6, 1776. On commissioners see *Penn. Packet,* February 26, 1776.
71. *Penn. Eve. Post.*
72. Ibid., March 2, 1776.

73. This essay first appeared in *The Pennsylvania Ledger: or the Virginia, Maryland, Pennsylvania, & New-Jersey Weekly Advertiser* and was soon reprinted in the other papers. This essay and many others that were printed in the papers after this date have been reproduced in volume five of Peter Force, ed., *American Archives: Fourth Series* . . . (Washington, D.C.: M. St. Clair Clarke and Peter Force, 1844) (hereafter cited as Force, ed., *Am. Arch.:* 4th ser.). For the ease of the reader, I shall cite this work rather than the original newspaper where possible.

74. David Hawke suggests that the committee limited itself to the issue of representation. See his *In the Midst of a Revolution* (Philadelphia: University of Pennsylvania Press, 1961), p. 22 (hereafter cited as Hawke, *Midst*). It has been suggested that representation was not at all important, but that the drive to independence was the key to the committee's action. See Richard A. Ryerson, "Leadership in Crisis: The Radical Committees of Philadelphia and the Coming of the Revolution in Pennsylvania, 1765–1776: A Study in the Revolutionary Process" (Ph. D. dissertation, Johns Hopkins University, 1973), pp. 494–95 (hereafter cited as Ryerson, "Leadership").

75. *Penn. Statutes*, 8:459–62.

76. J. Paul Selsam, *The Pennsylvania Constitution of 1776: A Study in Revolutionary Democracy* (Philadelphia: University of Pennsylvania Press, 1936), pp. 31–39 and Charles H. Lincoln, *The Revolutionary Movement in Pennsylvania, 1760–1776* (Philadelphia: University of Pennsylvania Press, 1901), pp. 42–52.

77. "An Elector," in Force, ed., *Am. Arch.:* 4th ser., pp. 1118–19. See also sources in note 78.

78. For the view that this was the case especially where the question of representation was concerned, see Selsam, *Pennsylvania Constitution*, pp. 99–100 and Lincoln, *Revolutionary Movement*, pp. 51–52.

79. On the "moderates," see Hawke, *Midst*, pp. 13–31 and passim. "Cato's" second letter first appeared on February 13 (*Penn. Gazette*). Smith may have known then that an expansion in the Assembly and thus an election were coming soon. For his seven essays that appeared between the 13th and the election on May 1, see Force, ed., *Am. Arch.:* 4th ser., pp. 188–90, 443–46, 514–17, 542–46, 839–43, 850–53, 1049–50. For other writings of the moderates that appeared or were submitted to the press before the May election, see Ibid., pp. 802–03, 1036–38, 1140–43; "Aesop," *Penn. Gazette*, April 3, 1776; "Moderator," *Pennsylvania Ledger*, April 27, 1776.

80. For an excellent listing and discussion of the "radicals," see Ryerson, "Leadership," especially pp. 332–39, 466–83. The major radical writings were by James Cannon and Tom Paine. See Force, ed., *Am. Arch.:* 4th ser., pp. 431–34, 529–31, 828–34, 921–26, 1016–20, 1092–94. Of the other radical writers, and there were many separate signatures, the best examples of viciousness and stress on economic issues are: "Old Trusty," *Penn. Eve. Post*, March 19 and April 30, 1776; "[To] Mr. Towne," Ibid., April 27, 1776; "Proposals . . .," *Postscript* to *Penn Packet*, April 8, 1776.

81. Anne Bezanson, *Prices and Inflation During the American Revolution: Pennsylvania, 1770–1790* (Philadelphia: University of Pennsylvania Press, 1951), p. 30.

82. *Penn. Journal*, February 24, 1776.

83. *Penn. Eve. Post*, March 7, 1776.

84. Ibid.

85. Ryerson ("Leadership") does a very good job of showing the role of the activists. On the question of the "inarticulate," see Jesse Lemisch and John K. Alexander, "The White Oaks, Jack Tar, and the Concept of the 'Inarticulate'," *William and Mary Quarterly*, 3rd ser., 29 (July 1972) :109–34 and especially pp. 130–34.

86. Quotation from "Cato" in Force, ed., *Am. Arch.:* 4th ser., p. 189 with emphasis added. See also sources in note 93.

87. Quotation from Hawke, *Midst*, p. 35 and see also pp. 33–35. Ryerson ("Leadership," pp. 529–31) agrees with this view.

88. *Penn. Statutes*, 2:213–14 and Albert E. McKinley, *The Suffrage Franchise in the Thirteen English Colonies in America* (Philadelphia: published for the University of Pennsylvania, 1905), pp. 285–92.

89. *Penn. Statutes*, 2:212–21; 4:77–80, 375–81; 5:16–22; 7:32–40. Election inspectors were so important that they were slated. See Marshall, *Diary*, p. 67, entry of April 25, 1776.

90. Hawke was not sure if the election was confined to the legally defined city (*Midst*, pp. 34–35, note 6). The wording of the election laws and the fact that votes were cast only at the city polling place and not at the "suburban" polling places suggests that the election was confined to the legally defined city. See e.g., *Penn. Packet*, May 6, 1776 and cf. *Penn. Statutes*, 7:32, 33.

91. Alexander, "Philadelphia's 'Other Half'," pp. 45–51.

92. *Memoirs*, pp. 119, 265. It is worth noting that Hawke (*Midst*, p. 208) praises Graydon's *Memoirs* as being "the best single account" of the city's "social scene" in 1776. For the statements of others of the day who support Graydon's view, see [James Clitherall], "Extracts from the Diary of Dr. James Clitherall, 1776," *PMHB* 22 (No. 4, 1898) :469 (hereafter cited as Clitherall, "Diary"); Scharf and Westcott, *History*, 1:321, note 1.

93. Elizabeth Drinker, *Extracts from the Journal of Elizabeth Drinker*, Henry D. Biddle, ed. (Philadelphia: J. B. Lippincott, 1889), p. 45; Marshall, *Diary*, pp. 69–70; *Penn. Journal*, May 15, 1776.

94. Quotations from Edmund C. Burnett, *The Continental Congress* (New York: Macmillan, 1941), pp. 157, 158 and Adams, *Works*, 2:510.

95. Clitherall, "Diary," pp. 469–70; Marshall, *Diary*, pp. 72–73; Scharf and Westcott, *History*, 1:312.

96. Scharf and Westcott, *History*, 1:312; *Penn. Gazette*, June 12, 1776; Selsam, *Pennsylvania Constitution*, p. 132; Harold D. Eberlin and Cortland Van Dyke Hubbard, *Diary of Independence Hall* (Philadelphia: J. B. Lippincott, 1948), p. 169.

97. Selsam, *Pennsylvania Constitution*, pp. 136–45 and the Proceedings of the meeting, which are in *Penn. Statutes*, 9:468–500 with quotation from p. 499.

98. Eberlin and Cortland, *Diary*, p. 171.

99. Ibid., pp. 175–80 and quotations from Marshall, *Diary*, p. 83; Scharf and Westcott, *History*, 1:321, note 1.

100. Marshall, *Diary*, pp. 81–83 and Selsam, *Pennsylvania Constitution*, p. 146.

101. *Penn. Statutes*, 9:473–75 passim.

102. Selsam, *Pennsylvania Constitution*, pp. 146–47 and Ryerson, "Leadership," p. 604.

103. Francis N. Thorpe, *The Federal and State Constitutions . . .*, 7 vols. (Washington, D.C.: Government Printing Office, 1909), gives the 1776 Constitution (5:3081–92 with quotations on p. 3088) and the basic frame of government of 1701 (Ibid., pp. 3076–81).

104. Quotation from *Penn. Statutes*, 9:65 and see also Edward P. Allinson and Boies Penrose, *Philadelphia 1681–1887: A History of Municipal Development* (Philadelphia: Allen, Lane and Scott, 1887), pp. 3, 8–9, 52–59.

105. Bezanson, *Prices*, p. 30; *Penn. Gazette*, June 10 and October 8, 1776.

106. *Penn. Gazette*, August 27 and see also August 13, 1776.

107. Quotations and tone of the times from Marshall, *Diary*, pp. 103–06, 195–97; see also Eberlin and Hubbard, *Diary*, pp. 203–09.

108. Quotation from Marshall, *Diary*, p. 103 and on the military action see Don Higginbotham, *The War of American Independence: Military Attitudes, Policies, and Practice, 1763–1789* (New York: Macmillan, 1971), pp. 165–71. The British *did* come in 1777 but the city, while slightly worse for the visit, was not

destroyed. See Eberlin and Hubbard, *Diary,* p. 238 and Scharf and Westcott, *History,* 1:349ff.

109. Brown, *King's Friends,* pp. 129–53.

110. Allinson and Penrose, *Philadelphia,* pp. 52–59.

111. These complaints and the story of the battle over the Constitution of 1776 are told in Robert L. Brunhouse, *The Counter-Revolution in Pennsylvania 1776–1790* (Harrisburg: Pennsylvania Historical Commission, 1942).

112. This "Dialogue" appeared in *Penn. Eve. Post,* October 10, 15, 17, 19, 24, 31, 1776 with all quotations from the issue of the 24th. This essay, which Marshall (*Diary,* p. 95) called a "severe Satire," was probably the work of one person. And he did not like the Constitution of 1776. Thus he may have had "Orator" —whose name was also given as "Puff"—say things he hoped would turn people against the Constitution. But there were persons in the city who held views similar to those of the "Orator," as shown by Selsam *(Pennsylvania Constitution,* pp. 187–88, 205–11) and John N. Shaeffer, "Public Consideration of the 1776 Pennsylvania Constitution," *PMHB* 98 (October 1974), pp. 423-25.

113. For an examination of some of the immediate effects on the Philadelphia of 1780-1800, see John K. Alexander, "The City of Brotherly Fear . . .," in *Cities in American History,* Kenneth T. Jackson and Stanley K. Schultz, eds. (New York: Knopf, 1972), pp. 79-97.

PHILADELPHIA 1876

Celebration and Illusion

DENNIS CLARK

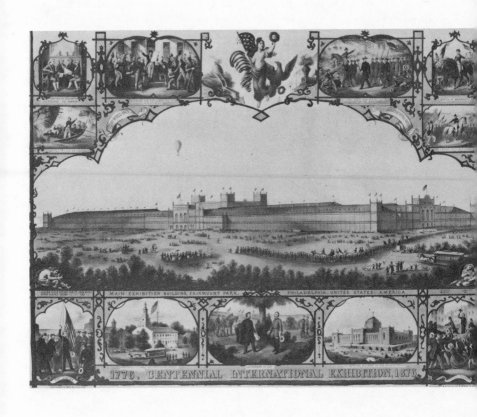

Centennial International Exhibition with scenes from the
nation's history. Lithograph by H. Schile (courtesy of the
New York Historical Society, New York City)

Throughout his classic *Democracy in America,* Alexis de Tocqueville repeatedly expresses his fear that the private passions and pursuits of Americans will lead them to lose sight of their best interests and social well-being.[1] An examination of Philadelphia in the period of the Centennial Exposition of 1876 provides us with a study of a city eager to flatter its passions at the expense of its own best interests. For men entering the third century of life in the American republic, the study of our cities in the past may show just why it is that problems of urban decay and confusion in our own time are so intractable and defiant. The long tradition of exploitation and disorderly development of American cities has been one of the chief weaknesses of our democracy, and the industrial Philadelphia of the 1870's gives many clues as to why this has been so.

The men who had exalted democracy in the red brick eighteenth century city of Philadelphia were marvels of optimistic nationalism. They saw reason and science as guides to a social contract with the future. The American Revolution was sufficiently conservative so that its leaders expected the future to conserve it. On the one hand there was a rationalist design for the republic almost geometric in its balance of state and federal functions, the whole made chaste in political dignity through the attribution of Athenian virtues. On the other hand was the romantic elevation of the citizen into a paragon of political aspirations. The unity of citizen probity and republican institutions was novel and splendid and was expected to progress toward perfection in triumph over the tumultuous and arrant contentions of pioneer America.[2]

Philadelphia, where this singular experiment in nationalism was launched in 1776, was itself fully expressive of the values upon which the American leaders sought to found their republican institutions. Its rectangular street plan and modestly proportionate colonial building design testified to rationalistic order. Its history as a haven for dissent and Quaker experiment manifested the romantic religious spirit liberated by the Enlightenment. Following the disruptions of the Revolution, the traditional whiggish leadership of the city reasserted itself to preside over expanding horizons of prosperity, ordered governance and intelligent progress. The busy port, the meetings at the State House at Fifth and Chestnut Streets, the deliberations of the American Philosophical Society stimulated the life of the city under these values. That the leaders of the Revolution and the framers of republican institutions had been largely anti-urban and oblivious of the possibility of an urban future was not evident until some generations later.[3]

That profuse irregularity set in motion by the disruptions of the American Revolution has been well documented by Gordon Wood, John Alexander and others, and the impulse to diversity did become one of the major forces in nineteenth century development.[4] This had profound implications for the great port cities, which were the hinges of American power. As the cities became glutted with ever more people, more commerce and industry, the chaste values of the nation's founders became distorted in the attempt to make them fit a society for which they had not been originally cast. The leadership of the cities became first confused, then despairing and finally cynical. The democracy of yeomen and tidy burghers envisioned by the founders became the raving mass democracy of the urban political machine, with its polyglot tainted rewards. Leaders turned to industry as the temples of republican veneration rocked under the impact of pluralist contest. The institutions of the eighteenth century, with their simple and classical facades, were increasingly seen to be inadequate to the burgeoning needs of a suffering urban populace that had more direct ties with the gloomy bulk of the city's factories. What had the American Philosophical Society to say to the teacher struggling with three dozen immigrant children? What had the revered portraits on the State House walls to say to the citizen whose vote was sold by his ward leader? How could the old Almshouse and the Friends' Yearly Meeting deal with ten thousand unemployed? The new urban reality threatened to strangle the freedom that had summoned it into existence.

PURSUIT OF PRODUCTION

In the 1870's the city of Philadelphia was a labyrinth of labor and technology, and its chroniclers loved to enumerate the vastness of its industrial innovation. A souvenir booklet about the incongruous visit of some Japanese notables to the city in 1872 would not have been complete without its appendix cataloguing the city's proud elements: 125,000 buildings, 300 miles of paved streets, 86,000 gas lights, 8,339 businesses churning out 335 million dollars worth of production annually. In its chapter on the industries of Philadelphia, the history of the city being compiled in the 1870's by J.

Thomas Scharf and Thompson Westcott would boastfully itemize the rolling
mills, saw foundaries, wire mills, stove works, soap factories, distilleries,
brickyards, flour mills, huge textile and carpet factories and vast profusion
of workshops, stores and warehouses that were crammed into the maze of
masonry of the city. Within this fastness of energy and structures there lived
by 1870 some 675,000 people, and by 1880 the population would increase
by another 160,000.[5]

The modest Quaker town that had been nurtured in Georgian elegance in
Benjamin Franklin's time had by the 1870's spread across the whole area for
five miles above the point where the Delaware and Schuylkill Rivers met.
The valleys of each of the rivers were now laced with railroad tracks, and a
canal wended up the Schuylkill. Throughout the area most people still lived
close to work places. Rows of brick houses were ranked block after block
around four- and five-story factories.[6] Neighborhoods were a mixture of
housing, little stores, stables and a bewildering miscellany of mill yards, lofts,
pens, sidings and piles of coal, refuse and lumber. The Census of 1870
showed the average family to have more than five members, and an average
dwelling unit more than six occupants.[7] In the small row houses in which
most of the city's more than 200,000 workers lived, that new invention, the
convertible sofa bed, known as the "Murphy bed," was a welcome space
saver.

Although outlying areas of the city still retained rural vestiges, especially
in the hilly woods above Germantown and in the broad fields in West Philadelphia and beyond the mills of Frankford Creek in the northeast part of
the county, the intensity of urban aggregation could be seen most readily in
center city. William Penn's plan of rectangles and measured geometry was
now partitioned in a thousand ways through every artifice known to the real
estate manipulator and the legal conveyancer. Through an incessant process
of development, the center city had begun to take on the giantism that was
to characterize technical urbanism. The convenient residential ambience
that had been part of the early nineteenth century city east of Broad Street
had been altered. The leading families living on Arch Street, South Fourth
through Thirteenth Streets and on the gracious streets named for the lovely
native trees, Chestnut, Walnut, Locust, Spruce and Pine, had moved or were
thinking of doing so. They moved west of Broad Street, or to Chestnut Hill
or other sylvan refuges.[8]

In the former residential precincts, the commercial city now reigned.
Chestnut Street was increasingly the location of banks, insurance companies,
publishers and corporations of every description. Market Street, the main

east-west axis, had early become commercialized, but now all the side streets were as well. The huge Public Ledger Building at Sixth and Walnut Streets loomed over Independence Square. John Wanamaker's store at Sixth and Market Streets, worth the then awesome sum of $250,000, symbolizing expanding retail trade.

It would be difficult to exaggerate the practical and symbolic importance of the new central city's composition. The dominant elements of the new commercial core were the edifices of money, retail trade and entertainment. Even in the face of the depression of 1873, the banks of Philadelphia produced a record of financial growth and strength. The financial system was flawed with the gambler's optimism that touched all the enterprise of the day. By 1873 there were twice as many banks in the city as there had been in 1859. Everywhere new state and local banks seemed to emerge. To the ranks of the august Girard Bank and the Philadelphia National Bank were added lusty giants like the Farmers' and Mechanics' Banks. The latter had the advantage of being fiscal agent for the Commonwealth of Pennsylvania. After the city treasurer was caught in illegal speculations in 1871, it became agent for the city government as well. The largest bank to default in the 1870's was the Fourth National, when its troubles deepened early in the decade as a result of the defalcations of its cashier. Thievery, bank robberies and speculative vertigo charged the growth of the banks with the uncertain spirit of the times.[9]

Another source of the city's capitalization with great impact on its residential development were the "people's banks," savings and loan associations into which working people put their weekly mites and created for themselves sources of mortgage money for their housing needs. Millions in mortgage funds were loaned annually through these organizations, especially to immigrants, whose ethnic ties helped promote the funds.[10] Thus, a source of credit was opened to workers who would not have been able to borrow from regular banks because of their lack of collateral. Much of the popular row house building of the time was carried out on the basis of this system of savings pools. Unfortunately, these associations also developed reputations for dishonesty and default.

If the financial core of the city along east Walnut Street represented the true complexity of a metropolis, so did the burgeoning retail network. Because of the mass-produced clothing made possible by the widespread adoption of the sewing machine, clothing sales became much simplified with ready-to-wear articles after the Civil War. Then the diversity of production of the new manufacturing system poured forth. Fabrics by the roll, flatirons by the gross, Mason jars by the box, lace curtains and even a hideaway "Centennial Bed" became widely available. Storekeepers shifted from specializing in the sale of one item to sale of a whole range of products.[11] The venerable stores like Bailey and Company in jewelry and J. E. Caldwell in handsome plate limited themselves, but newer firms sold diversity. They also became much more preoccupied with display, with long front windows and bigger glass cases. Diversity and display became the chief assets of downtown retailers, and they pushed their advantages until their stores became synonymous with the central city.

A further element in the new "downtown" was the increased entertainment there. The area around Eighth and Walnut Street was one focus of dramatic delights. The elegant and historic Walnut Theater dominated this area. On South Broad Street from Spruce Street to Walnut was another array of "museums," lecture rooms and concert halls. In the magnificent sweep of the golden balconies of the Academy of Music, the city's elite would rank themselves in gem-bedecked finery for recitals and operatic performances. Mrs. John Drew's Arch Street Theater formed the nucleus north of Market Street for what would become the city's most popular entertainment district later in the century.[12] This commercial entertainment activity rounded out the cosmopolitan attractions of the central city, giving life there a quality unmatched anywhere else in the entire commonwealth.

But close by the financial, retail and entertainment establishments was the intrusive industrialism that was the city's backbone. The clanging sheet metal factory of Alan Wood was at Fifth and Arch and the Johnson Type Foundry at Sixth and Sansom. The lack of concerted planning was blatantly obvious. The center city with its webs of telegraph wires, racing message boys, clouds of wagon dust—in which there were, in turn, clouds of manure dust—and the jumble of board fences, steps and sheds behind stone-fronted buildings all betrayed the essentially uncontrolled aggrandizement with which the city grew.

This collectivity of services and businesses in center city made up on a newly enlarged scale a series of urban worlds through which the citizen could pass with convenience. From the exciting speculations of the money markets, one could move through the artful displays of the fine shops or attend a melodrama at a theater. Specially cultivated tropical gardens, exhibits of Asian treasures and publicly performed scientific experiments vied for attention. A model of the "Centennial City" at the Colosseum at Broad and Locust Street drew people by the hundreds to see for the first time the entire prospect of their city of Philadelphia spread out before them in delightful miniature.[13] All this artifice made the center city more beguiling than ever before, despite its problems and discomforts. It was a seemingly endless plenitude of novelty and sensations, and people could lose themselves in its miles of windowed streets.

The energized concentration in the center of Philadelphia was only part of the city's strenuous expansion, however. If the center gave the city its most notable features as a metropolis, its residential neighborhoods gave it the distinctive domestic quality that was to become fixed in the popular ideas of the city. The relatively flat topography of the area between the city's two rivers became a battleground for a generation that saw "the community as real estate."[14] The surveying of plats and parcels went on with furious disregard for the natural hindrances. Creeks were bricked over, springs stifled, the land leveled, trees abolished and grass and bush reduced to macadam and cobblestone byways. This was the age in which the mass of the city's population lost that precious bounty of green and breathing nature that had induced Penn to call his colony sylvan. The mechanics of urban overbuilding were perfected in the 1870's, and the resulting encasement of the city's outer areas in brick density, with here and there a pathetic green survival, overwhelmed the natural endowment of neighborhoods. Even in the steep areas of Manayunk and the Falls of the Schuylkill with their thirty-degree grades, the mills and row houses marched in lines up the slopes. The majority of Philadelphians were housed in the rigidity of rows, and the last opportunities to make birdsong and the scent of sap part of the memory-store of city children faded.

If the row house areas of North Philadelphia and West Philadelphia promised a future of neighborhood life lived almost exclusively in rectangular dimensions, the older housing districts extended a tradition of misery going back to colonial Philadelphia. There were notorious streets in the Alaska district near Sixth and Lombard Street that were classic slums. The spaces behind row houses were built over with additional box-like structures. These alley dwellings, with outdoor pumps and privies, existed by the thousands in the 1870's and were a scourge to the health and well-being of the poor, especially blacks and newly arrived immigrants. In older neighborhoods like Southwark, ramshackle wood and jerry-built brick buildings were jumbled among stables, piggeries and work sheds. Conditions were little better along the banks of the Schuylkill near Gray's Ferry and along the Delaware in Kensington and Port Richmond, where coal heavers and dock wallopers eked out a hard living when they got work. Other sections of North and South Philadelphia were mere shanty towns. The 1870's were a decade too early for even the small housing reform activities of Helen Parrish and the Octavia Hill Association, which sought to obtain fair rents and minimum levels of decency. The slum, then, expanded, more crowded than ever, and more dangerous than previously. It was one neighborhood configuration that mocked the Centennial pride of Philadelphia in all the older sections of the city.[15]

Still the pride of the city was not wanting among the wealthy families, whose names crowded the lists of directors of the most prestigious businesses and institutions. Their homes formed another kind of Philadelphia neighborhood far from the slums. Chestnut Hill was the preëminent haven. Here the eclectic architecture of the Gilded Age created huge castles, lavishly decorated mansions, Tudor lodges, Georgian country houses, baronial Queen Anne creations with peaked roofs and pointed towers, extraordinary and frequently tasteless testimonies to flagrant wealth. The opening of the Reading Railroad's new line to Chestnut Hill in 1854 made the wooded area accessible to the socially prominent. H. H. Houston built eighty houses there, as well as "Druim Moir," his own mansion. "Greystock" housed the family of George C. Thomas of Drexel and Company. Mr. Chancellor English moved into the rambling opulence of "Norwood Hall." The estates, ranging from imitation Gothic to French chateau, formed a verdant belt of wild architectural fancy, and names like "Evergreens," "Edgecombe," "Hope Lodge" and "Highlands" adorned them, making them seem like the dream dwellings that shop girls read about in romantic novels. And indeed, they were dream dwellings as far as the bulk of the city's population could know of them.[16]

Through all these areas steamed the railroads, imperious, the steel lifelines of the nation's largest single business. The railroads were one of the reasons for the city's industrial eminence. Some thirty-five miles of trackage was laid throughout the built-up areas of the city alone. This meant that contiguous to the railroads with their smoke and soot-spewing engines were over 800 of the city's residential blocks. The engines brought noise, dirt and respiratory dangers to 40,000 homes. The railroads brought more than prosperity to industries.[17]

SOCIAL FAILURES

Not only had the physical face of the city changed drastically, but the population of Philadelphia was now greatly diversified. The predominantly Anglo-Saxon character of the city had been offset by heavy immigration since the 1830's. By 1870, one out of four persons in the city was foreign born. There were almost 100,000 Irish-born in the city. There were 50,000 Germans. More blacks had been coming to the city since the Civil War. Crowded into the slums in South and North Philadelphia were thousands of people who could hardly speak English, who were often illiterate and whose families were wrenched daily by poverty and the confusion fostered by the demands of city living.[18] At a mass meeting of workers in 1876, labor leader Peter C. Maguire lamented that while the products of American workmen would be shown at the Centennial Exhibition, the suffering of immigrant workers would not.[19]

In the decade of the 1860's, when Philadelphia industry had experienced a war and postwar boom, the South Philadelphia wards had increased by 30,000 people, those in North Philadelphia by 50,000 and those in Kensington by 25,000.[20] These increases reflected the foreign influx, which was only a little more tolerable to the city in the 1870's than it had been in 1844 when anti-Irish Nativist riots had required martial law to restore peace. Between 1840 and 1870 the Roman Catholics alone had built thirty-three churches. The Jews dedicated a new synagogue, Rodeph Sholom, in 1870.[21] The industrial might of the city required laborers in massive numbers, but their labor had to be obtained amid religious, social and cultural differences that were deeply unsettling. The Germans were closely knit in their retention of German ways. The Irish, dominating the crime news of the daily papers, were constantly hatching wild schemes of revolutionary violence, such as the plots of the Fenian Brotherhood in 1866 for an Irish invasion of Canada. The *Philadelphia North American* had to reassure uneasy readers in 1876 in an editorial that "Cities like Philadelphia are hotbeds of effort, thought, progress, enterprise. . . ." and that they should not fear that too many worthy people were removing themselves from the city.[22]

Along with the changes in the physical configuration and demographic make-up of the city, there had also come a change in the social fabric of Philadelphia. The old whiggish oligarchies that had helped to usher the city into the age of machinery and mills had been outpaced by new men, a whole new race of entrepreneurs and promoters whose ideas of civic leadership were foreshortened by economic dictates. The social dislocations caused by the industrial economy and immigration created a new scale of restlessness. The first half of the nineteenth century had often been disruptive and riotous, but the effects were limited.[23] With the massed population of the post-Civil War period, the fear of unbridled disorder and class conflict grew. The riches of the industrial bourbons had surpassed anything dreamed of by the old tradition-oriented first families, and the sufferings of the poor had been hugely magnified. The social environment was actively hostile toward working people.[24] The resulting turbulence became a prominent feature of urban living.

Scharf and Westcott note that "The year 1871 was one of numerous disturbances, murderous assaults and other infractions of the peace."[25] Racial and political riots were common. Staid E. P. Oberholtzer of the University of Pennsylvania found that "Many classes of Philadelphians, including the editors of the *Press*, seem to have carried pistols habitually."[26] Such publications as the *Police Gazette, Day's Doings* and *Sporting Times* glorified violence and sensational crimes, lacing their stories with broadly suggestive material that was deemed salacious in the Victorian age.[27] The depression of 1873 added to the general anxiety as thousands became unemployed. Jay Cooke and his banking colleagues at dinner in his mansion in Chestnut Hill were insulated from the turbulence of the city. They had seen the fury of the Civil War and survived it, and they could set their teeth against the spreading distress that was eating at the vitals of the city.

To understand the Philadelphia of the 1870's, it is necessary to know the values that dominated it. Just as the rationalism and Enlightenment outlook of the patriot leaders of 1776 helps explain the eighteenth century drama that took place among Georgian porticos and neoclassic columns, so the ideas of the industrial age help explain the row dwellings packed among the mills and the life of the smoke-wreathed city of 1876. The most actively propagated belief animating the city in the 1870's was the faith in commerce and industry. The rationalist optimism and confidence in science of the eighteenth century had been transformed into a practical zeal and commitment to technology and commercial gain in the nineteenth. As J. L. Vansant stated in his illustrated history of successful business houses in the city in 1869, ". . . the Royal Road to Wealth is open to all. It is found in a careful study of the Lives of our Successful men. . . ." The philosophy of business success was aggressive. The *Philadelphia North American,* whose pages were packed with advertising and long articles on monetary theories, welcomed competition from other maritime cities. Its editorials trumpeted the technical and educational advantages of the city and stated flatly, "Wealth will cluster naturally in such a city."[28] In an age when religion held a special place in the minds and hearts of most Americans, Russell Conwell made a career out of declamations full of religious citations extolling wealth. "We ought to be rich because money has power," he intoned to rapt audiences.[29] He decried critics of wealth and equated the acquisition of money with religious betterment. The exaltation of property was the chief precept of the period.

What of people who had little or no property? Were they, too, mesmerized by its attractions? Indeed, most were. The novelty of a society based upon the production of unprecedented amounts of physical things had a notable impact on all classes. Though some might be embittered by want, most hoped for deliverance, for the Horatio Alger miracle. People by the thousands, only recently released from subsistence economies, found in the industrial city for all the suffering it entailed a seeming fulfillment or at least a promise of adequacy in worldly goods, and they believed the promise. Such people outweighed those inextricably caught amid the hope-draining contradictions of the wage slavery and destitution of the under class.

Undergirding the ethic of property and its religious substantiation was a hardy traditionalism embodied in the upper classes and strenuously imitated by the lower. Upon emerging from the Civil War, the nation needed to reaffirm its unity and its binding institutions. The Constitution, triumphant above secession now, was exalted by all. The Founding Fathers were uncritically idolized. The struggle of an America seeking the bounty of newly tapped resources in every state was manifest and satisfying. The achievements of the country confirmed its belief in itself. What was American was consecrated in popular esteem. The millions of new people in this new land were aware that there was indeed an American tradition and they were pledged to it. The prostrate South, the depression of 1873, the cruelties of the factory system did not gainsay this commitment to the mythic tradition of the country. And in Philadelphia, where the nation had been born and where its history was attested by numerous sites and institutions, the cult of constitutional and conservative reverence was strong.[30]

The leaders of the city who embodied the prevailing values were men of opportunity and, more often than not, raw opportunists. The robust new men of power in the city were not the descendants of the colonial magnates and eighteenth century worthies. Such families were still strongly represented in the banking and financial segments of the city's life, tidily husbanding wealth year after year. But the men changing the city through industrialism were individualist entrepreneurs who as a group constituted an aggressive plutocracy. Mathias Baldwin, king of the locomotive makers, Joseph Wharton of Bethlehem Iron Company, Charles Wheeler, William Sellers, Henry Disston and Samuel Merrick, all forgers of metal and of fortunes from metal. Thomas Dolan, who made the cloth sold by John Wanamaker, Justus Strawbridge and Isaac Clothier. Peter Widener and William L. Elkins, whose traction deals pyramided their millions. Morton McMichael, publisher and ally of wealth, praised unreservedly an array of men such as Henry Howard Houston and Thomas A. Scott, made notable by railroad riches.[31]

These men, masters of the mills and the power of the city, were newly rich. They built ostentatious mansions on North Broad Street and sought entry into the old Philadelphia Club and the new Racquet Club. Their fortunes from steel, the railroads and utilities were built into the structure of the city. The mythology of the self-made man may have been widely believed, and these men may have believed that they had been responsible for their own fortunes. The truth, of course, was that in an age of growing technical and economic complexity, the amassing of corporate capital and profits was inescapably a social phenomenon. Hordes of workers contributed to the enterprises these men headed; thousands more were related in a more remote way to the production systems as competitors, consumers, insurers and imitators. The business and industrial leaders had to be understood, however, according to a simpler imagery comprehensible to themselves and the public, hence the individualist stereotype. It is worth noting in this respect that the city leaders of the 1870's were not well-educated men.[32] As descendants of families launched in Philadelphia in the first half of the nineteenth century, they did not have a personal stake in the eighteenth century tradition of leadership through erudition.

The politics of the city did not much concern these business magnates. The Republican party, redolent with the laurels of Civil War victory, was superascendant in the city and the state. The key powers of incorporation, franchise and regulation of economic life belonged to the state, so that the Commonwealth received more attention than the city. The scandals of the Grant administration defaced the national political arena, so that state affairs were given even more attention than usual. The stalwart Republican citizens of Philadelphia had been handily composed into ranks of allegiance that were proof against electoral challenge from the emaciated Democratic party, still stained by affiliation with Southern rebellion. Machine bosses like William B. Mann and James McManes held sway over a rickety city government capped by the curiosity of a bicameral City Council. That council by 1876 was almost four to one Republicans over Democrats.[33] As with so many things in the city in the 1870's, political organization had really reached a form whose potential was not realized. The structure of the political machine was there, and it could have been used to deal more effectively with abounding problems and to express popular distress, but the requisite coherence was not imposed on it. What was true of politics was true of industry, education and institutions serving social needs.

Because of its industrial progress and expansion, Philadelphia had out-grown the institutions that had been charged with caring for its social prob-lems. The chronology of the establishment of agencies for what we would today call social welfare is revealing. When industrialization began in the 1830's, the eighteenth century Almshouse and such reformist institutions as the Eastern Penitentiary and the House of Refuge were already inadequate to the scale of need. Jefferson Medical College and the Philadelphia College of Pharmacy were still haplessly speculating about the causes of the recurrent cholera epidemics and such scourges as "childbed fever." The churches car-ried on an uneven charitable mission that was both cramped and evangelical.

With the arrival of the massive Irish immigrant influx in the 1840's, such a wave of destitution hit the city that a whole new range of institutions grew up to deal with poverty and attendant social problems. From this period date the growth of the Union Home for Children (1855), the Industrial Home for Girls (1859), the Home for Colored Children (1856), the Northern Home for Friendless Children (1854), the Institution for the Feeble Minded (1853), the Charity Hospital (1858), the old Municipal Hospital at 21st and Hart Lane (1855). These foundations of the 1850's after the first shock of mass immigration were a response on the part of the city to greater need. Refuges for "fallen women," shelters for itinerant workers, apprentice schemes, foster care programs and other activities reflected a Victorian paternalism. In addition, the immigrants themselves built a remarkable network of service institutions from their own meager resources. Catholic parishes were centers of neighborhood assistance. The Jewish Foster Home (1855), the German Hospital (1858) and St. Mary's Hospital (1866) each served its clientele.[34]

By the 1870's, however, the increasing population had again outpaced the facilities to deal with the social and physical injury inflicted on the poor and less competent by rampant industrialism. The Blockley Almshouse alone by 1876 had a population of 2,500 including 600 insane, and its budget was $250,000 annually. In a Centennial publication, Earl Shinn wrote that if the Almshouse, the Moyamensing Prison and other institutions were completely full, the slums of the city would still have a ". . . numerous, a riotous, a promiscuous, and a muck-begetting population of whites and blacks." It is worth notice that this writer, after describing soup kitchens and poverty pic-turesquely, turned quickly to the fountains and ordered privilege of Ritten-house Square and then devoted pages to extolling Stephen Girard as the model for men in the age of business.[35]

In the 1870's the leaders of Philadelphia were more intent upon endowing the city with monuments than succoring its unfortunate. In 1870 City Hall was begun, a massive French Renaissance extravaganza in stone. Across from the new City Hall, the towers of the Masonic Temple rose in newly completed elegance in 1873. At Broad and Cherry Street the Pennsylvania Academy of Fine Arts, opened in 1876, presented a rich facade to the passing coaches and horse cars. Horticultural Hall opened in 1867, the Mercantile Library in 1869.[36] Such institutions complemented well the new mansions that lined Broad Street, mansions with huge oak-paneled rooms, handsome carriage houses and troops of servants. Religious and civic leaders from the middle class by 1878 had founded the Philadelphia Society for Organizing Charity. Its goal was to reduce vagrancy and the number of paupers by a vigorous weeding out of "unworthy" poor. Its monthly visitors who checked up on recipients of charity were part of a federation that ". . . works upon the idea that true charity consists in giving only to the worthy."[37] Thus the development of the city's institutions for handling social distress was adumbrated. The making of monuments was ranked above ministering to one's fellow men.

Certainly one of the most critical problems of the city was education. According to the concepts of democracy, an educated electorate was highly important to public affairs. The leaders of industry affirmed the need in their work force for literate and disciplined employees. In a city that represented a new way of life full of technology and new urban forms, the number of people from simpler cultures was very large and the need to inform and guide them widespread. The drive to establish public schools, which had its roots in the eighteenth century, grew in the first half of the nineteenth century and led to unification of city schools, state standards of minimum requirements and rising enrollments. The pattern of private schools that represented the personal designs of single teachers who transformed themselves into school heads had faded. Religious denominations, however, had strengthened and expanded their networks of schools. The pre-Civil War school development had not met the rising needs, but it had vigor and promise.

After the Civil War, the problems of the schools deepened. The difficulty of administering a mass school system, a novel enterprise, became more evident every year. Politicians sought influence over the schools to dispense jobs and favors. Directors of schools were of dubious ability. The *Philadelphia North American* scornfully stated, "It is a fact that some school directors are not only illiterate but ill-bred, and illustrate only bad manners and bad grammar."[38] The conditions of school buildings gave rise to numerous complaints from parents. Noting the attractiveness of schools in other countries, the *Philadelphia Inquirer* reported in 1876 that "the inside of a barn was generally more attractive to children than the inside of a school-house,"[39] and that Philadelphia schools were characterized by "utter inefficiency."

In 1876 a special census had been taken in the city revealing that at least 20,000 youngsters between ages six and eighteen were neither in school nor employed.[40] Even with the enrollment they had, the schools could only manage by composing many classes of seventy children. The diversity of the urban population was such that the schools could not comprehend or serve it properly. Finances, skills, organization and public support were simply not up to the task. Thus, in this crucial area of social development in which a new generation of children had to be tutored in the ways of industrial urbanism, the chief medium for accomplishing the task was not equipped for it. Nor were the growing numbers of Catholic and other private schools equal to it. Their financial problems were a standing constraint, their curricula even narrower than the Victorian rigidities in public schools and their orientation toward the city even more confused. As the urban future unfolded before the children of the 1870's, their textbooks, teachers and school experience largely ignored it.

If social problems and school needs taxed the capacity of the city, the economic complex that was the heart of the city's life and the pride of its leaders was in deep trouble. The Civil War had resulted in the strengthening of numerous Philadelphia manufacturing firms, especially in heavy metals, machinery, railroad equipment and the textile, chemical and leather industries. But the economy of the 1870's was spasmodic in its growth and contractions. The decade began with a bitter strike of the city's 1,000 shipyard workers. The next year the entire tailoring industry was disrupted by a strike. In 1872 the laborers of the gas works struck, curtailing the city's gas supply. Besides such major strikes, there were dozens of walk-outs, lock-outs and slow-downs. Labor unions under law were still considered conspiracies in restraint of trade, but even if workers could not openly organize, they could wreak havoc on production by informal strikes and agitation.[41]

In 1873 the true weakness of the industrial economy was revealed. Behind the growing manufacturing system was a faction-ridden and wildly speculative financial whirligig that supplied the loans and sold the stocks and debentures to raise capital for industrial expansion. Money is a sufficiently abstract feature of society that it seems to attract many men who increasingly take leave of reality the more money they amass. Jay Cooke and a whole cohort of others were of such a character. The greater their speculations, the more their ambitions grew. Cooke was involved in fantastic schemes for railroad promotion in Canada when the giddily teetering structure of his banking empire lost one of its chief supports. One of his New York banks closed on September 18 and others collapsed in rapid succession. Panic followed. Credit dried up. The wheels stopped turning and businesses were paralyzed. In the ensuing depression workers faced several winters without adequate fuel, food or any effective relief, and by 1877 there were 50,000 unemployed in the city.[42]

The *Philadelphia North American,* ever the exponent of headlong economic competition, rejoiced in the demise of those businesses wrecked by the crisis, attributing their failure to imprudent expansion. "Two years of stagnation and hard times have about made a clean sweep of them all," the paper said.[43] The harsh faith in economic struggle resulted in an ethical code not unlike that of the gladiatorial arena. The human costs were barely alluded to in the business reportage of the times.

The human costs were soon made evident to the city. Wage cuts on the railroads set off a nationwide wave of strikes in 1877. In Philadelphia tension rose as angry workers milled on the street corners. In July riots broke out around the West Philadelphia depot of the Pennsylvania Railroad. The city was in turmoil, and the mayor called for U.S. Marines and troops to suppress spreading violence. Police administered fierce clubbings to a meeting of 200 strikers at Kelly's Hall at Eighth and Christian Streets and similar clashes took place across the city. Here, then, was the underside of the new industrialism. Hordes of unemployed, great silent suffering and intermittent rages of protest and violence. A grim undercurrent to the economic achievements on which the city prided itself.[45]

The crisis of organization and development in the areas described above was symptomatic of the strains under which the growing city labored generally. The city had grown so inordinately that it had outpaced its own ability to cope with the institutional elements upon which its orderly governance depended. Both technology and the organization of public services brought challenges that could be met only in haphazard fashion. Thus, the new bridge across Girard Avenue opened in 1874 did little to relieve the chaotic traffic jams on such streets as Ridge Avenue. Cumbersome horse cars, brewery wagons, carriages and hand carts were clogged together in a tangle of animal and vehicle in streets laid out in the eighteenth century when such traffic was unforeseen. The city's early good record for insuring a decent water supply was only a memory by 1870. Though new pumping stations were put into service in that year, there were still extensive water shortages, and the pollution of the supplies drawn from the Delaware and Schuylkill Rivers constantly threatened the city with disease.[45] The city had to threaten prosecution to keep butchers from tossing their tons of offal into the sewer system, which frequently lacked drain grates and separate conduits for heavy rain run-off.[46] Though the old independent fire companies, which had long been a source of rioting, political thuggery and inefficient fire fighting, were at last superceded in 1871 by a new municipal fire department, the new service was far from adequate. With thousands of wooden buildings in the city, fires tended to be swift, big and persistent. The gas works set up in 1835 had become a sink of corruption. It was independent of the city, and a move to put it under full public control in 1868 failed. In the early 1870's, Mayor William S. Stokely, elected on a reform ticket, tried to fight the "Gas Ring" and lost. His administration later bogged down in its own corruption.[47]

The formation of the Citizens Municipal Reform Association in 1871 by Henry C. Lea was a feeble attempt to drive at least some of the local corruption out, but the corruption simply became more deeply embedded. Some historians have asserted that the only way to get things done by local government in the prevailing conditions was by widespread bribery, for bribery and payoffs were one means of organizing otherwise random forces.[48] The overriding problem was that the city was unprepared legally, financially and administratively to deal with novel problems. In order to control the proliferation of such things as telegraph and utility poles, the city had to go to court to establish its right to control the use of streets.[49] In order to fund its schools, the city had to depend on the state. In order to reduce the chaotic competition of traction lines, the city had to wait until the 1880's when William Elkins and Peter B. Widener imposed their own exploitive monopoly on city transit systems. As Sam Bass Warner has written, "The failure of Jay Cooke's generation and later generations of businessmen to take responsiblity for the consequences of the scale and organization of their business has turned their personal benevolence to ashes."[50]

The city budget for 1873 was $11,700,000 and rising rapidly. For 1874 it was projected to be $12,600,000 but actually reached $13,300,000.[51] The Commonwealth of Pennsylvania reacted to the escalation of urban growth and costs by attempting to assert more power over cities in the new state constitution adopted in 1873, but it placed a nefarious constraint on the cities by decreeing equality of taxation for all citizens no matter where they lived in the state.[52] This proscription baffled attempts to meet the cost differential inherent in administering urban areas. An act of the Pennsylvania General

Assembly in 1874 set up three classes of cities by population size, and this tended to set the major cities apart for invidious treatment by a preponderantly rural legislature. The inadequacy of the state's approach to Philadelphia's problems was signalized when the governor actually proposed a plan to break larger cities into huge conglomerations of tiny villages at a time when the Quaker City's population was nearly 800,000.[53]

CENTENNIAL DELIRIUM

It is in the light of this background that the great project for celebration of the Centennial of American independence must be viewed. Philadelphia, cradle of the nation-spawning events of 1776, exerted itself powerfully to celebrate the events in 1876. As early as 1870, the Centennial was anticipated in talks among city leaders.[54] Great exhibitions were something of a craze among governments in the mid-nineteenth century. Queen Victoria had opened the Crystal Palace exhibit in 1851, and Philadelphia firms had been represented at the Paris Exhibitions in 1855 and 1867. In 1871 the U.S. Congress set up a Centennial Commission with nationwide representation, and two years later the Philadelphia City Councils voted $25,000 to spur planning. By this time $1,700,000 was pledged to the Centennial from various sources. Philadelphia worried about the adequacy of its hotel facilities but otherwise plunged ahead with schemes for a vast deployment of festival facilities on no less than 450 acres of the city's spacious Fairmount Park.[55] This park, a truly remarkable preserve, was one of the great features of the city. It was essentially the result of the assembly of fine mansion grounds and estates along the Schuylkill River, and was an ideal site for a grand exhibition.

In harmony with the spirit of the times, the group that would preside over the affairs of the celebration was entitled The Board of Finance. John Welsh, a prominent commission merchant was president; William Sellers, an iron and steel tycoon, was vice-president. The ubiquitous John Wanamaker, Clement Biddle, N. Parker Shortridge, the super-energetic Frederick Fraley and other city notables generated enthusiasm as part of the board. The national Centennial Commission was headed by the Hon. Joseph R. Hawley of Massachusetts, and a Women's Committee under the redoubtable Mrs. E. D. Gillespie battled its way to a role in the event against stern male prejudice. A key figure in the promotional drive to build support for the celebration was John W. Forney, publisher and publicist, a tireless booster of the city who had visited

Europe to obtain information about how the huge exhibitions there had been organized.[56] It is worthy of note that this leadership did not include representation of the huge immigrant population thronging the city, to whom celebrating American independence would presumably have no little appeal.

Three years before the opening of the Centennial celebration, an alert Philadelphia publisher was printing a tabloid called *Crotzer's Centennial and Journal of the Exhibition.* In it were views of the exposition grounds and buildings in preparation, floor plans, bridge designs, decorations, activities of the Women's Committee and a plethora of details about the preparations. Befitting the home city of the Pennsylvania Railroad, a new depot was being built at the exposition site.[57] Special visitors' guides were in rapid preparation. Hotels and boarding houses were spruced up, and thousands of jobless Philadelphians looked for work connected with the great enterprise.

At last the momentous day of emotion arrived on May 10, 1876, when President U. S. Grant was to open the Exposition. Workmen still bustled to complete final tasks as the musicians practiced the special Centennial Inauguration March composed by Richard Wagner. A day that began rainy turned to blazing spring sunshine as 100,000 people moved to the Exposition grounds, where the President and Emperor Dom Pedro of Brazil joined in the opening ceremonies. America was on display in a gigantic fair of crenulated constructions. Buildings erected by major nations contained their wares and arts. Handicraft, artisan skill, artistic design and industrial prowess from throughout the world was revealed to the staring crowds. Cast iron canopies, glass-roofed vaults, tin-spired halls and soaring convolutions of carpenter's gothic carving welcomed the milling spectators. The huge Corliss engine, a monster symbol of industrial energy, attracted hordes of viewers. The Women's Pavilion included a steam engine operated by a female engineer as well as displays of needlework and domestic arts. Along with all this, the souvenir industry had outdone itself in a bounty of massproduced gimcracks. Never was Victorian bric-a-brac more lavishly produced. Fans, flags, scarves, doilies, aprons, plates, glasses, crewel samplers, pipes, baskets, combs and coins all tricked out with Centennial images and slogans feted the grand occasion.[58]

If the Exposition itself was a mighty display for the 9 million people who paid more than $11 million to see it, the rhetoric of the event was even more extraordinary. In an age of bombast, the Centennial Exposition opened floodgates of oratory and editorial exaggeration. Philadelphia was lauded for its "temples of arts and sciences" that "teem with the trophies of our moral and intellectual triumphs." The Exposition was "glorious in the seed . . . . more

glorious as we see it now full flowered."[59] The self-congratulatory sentiments that flowed forth were not in the least compromised by restraint.
The *Philadelphia North American* saluted the Centennial of independence
with a burst of patriotic tribute: "The central and whitest glory of this occasion is that all of the cardinal doctrines entering the original purpose have
been maintained, enlarged and improved by the experiment of a century."[60]
The paper praised the nation's founders for making general education the
support of popular government, and for uniting individual freedom and industrial power in a system that swept across the continent, freed the slaves,
gave refuge to the oppressed and fostered intellectual growth.

The guidebooks to the Exposition, the addresses of visiting dignitaries,
the memorial books and programs all proclaimed the glory of the nation and
all its works with heavy hyperbole. The *Philadelphia Inquirer* provided a
typical example on July 4, 1876: "For a century we have been proving our
manhood, proving our right to be free and independent states by victories
over enemies, foreign and domestic, by victories over climate, earth and
water."[61] The editorial went on to praise the clearing of forests, the invention of the locomotive and telegraph "to annihilate time and space," "the
printing press to educate mankind," "the sewing machine to emancipate
women" and "free homes" for immigrants.[62] It is little wonder that Herman
Melville found the Centennial to be "a tremendous Vanity Fair."[63]

The language of these declamations is important. It tells us a great deal
about the spirit of the age and emphasizes the contradictions inherent in a
huge public celebration in the midst of a problem-filled, depression-wracked
city. The euphoric Centennial statements idealized the American Revolution
and the American experience. They stressed the material successes of the
nation and ignored or played down Indian wars, secession, economic hardship and social divisions. These popular panegyrics were based upon assumptions that gratified and flattered Americans. They restated pieties that re-
assured a people that had been torn by Civil War. "America is good. We are
its people. Our deeds are good and they have led us to national glory, progress
and prosperity." That the facts of history were not so patently benign mat-
tered not. The first step in the service of an ideal is to state it. If the rhetoric
was specious, the unlettered immigrant and the general population of limited
education would not notice. The important thing was that the rhetoric of
Centennial celebration was politically unifying, socially flattering and psycho-
logically reassuring in a time of great change.[64]

Yet this eulogistic rhetoric betrays an immaturity, a fallacious public pos-
turing that was deeply discordant in itself. John Maass in his book on the

Centennial Exposition notes that one of the real achievements of the event was that it created a whole environment of buildings, displays, services and conveniences for acres and acres. It was an environment of illusion, the illusion of inevitable progress, and the public loved it.[65] Technology had made it possible to make dream fairs on a new and enlarged scale. All unwittingly the Centennial Exposition ushered into popular affection one of the main resources of modern mass society, the contrivance of extensive environments of illusion. The media of illusion, institutionalized in the cities in the form of parks, theater districts, stylized residential districts and public events of many kinds, enthralled the populace and served to bind together a citizenry of unprecedented diversity. The Centennial Exposition organized a new dimension for the democratic cult of civic adulation and nationalistic flattery in America. Philadelphia, the site of the great Exposition, like most problem-filled industrial cities, certainly needed reassurance in 1876 and thereafter.

If the Philadelphia of 1876 represents certain contradictions with respect to the ideas and social composition it inherited from 1776, it also displays to the historical inquirer contradictions within itself. The size, physical structure and dominant attitudes of the city were attributable in 1876 to the Industrial Revolution. The economic base prompted by industrialization was the city's chief boast, but controlling the development and effects of that economic base was its chief problem. To salute the great scientific and technological achievements of the nation in a Centennial extravaganza was one thing; to shape those achievements so that they were coordinated with the common good was quite another.

The Industrial Revolution and its opportunities, and the dream of America itself, had attracted multitudes of immigrants. The challenges of cultural assimilation, or at least balance, and the cleavages of class grew amid the fundamental difficulties of American life. The fact that Philadelphia historically would have a smaller foreign-born population than many other major American cities really did not relieve the strain greatly, for the city continued to have an upper class that was almost wilfully set against the passing of its leadership prerogatives.

Finally, the nature of the economy and community developed in the nineteenth century city prevented the exercise of restraint in dealing with the natural resources and real estate property in the built-up areas. There was no system for assessing depreciation and little accounting that could be legally defined concerning the wanton abuse and neglect of structures and amenities. Nor was there any mechanism for inducing reinvestment as the physical quality of the older city districts deteriorated. Age of structures became one of the key indices of decay. This incapacity of the city to conserve itself led eventually to enormous waste and social debility.

Philadelphia in 1876 was a sprawling laboratory of technological urbanism. Although many of the experiments conducted in the laboratory were profitable and proximately efficient, the overall conduct of the enterprise was so disorderly and misguided that the passage of time would simply increase the public costs imposed by energetic private initiatives. Economic fragmentation and harmfully delimited business responsibility, deep social divisions, and a lack of sensible physical management would become the legacy of the nineteenth century to the twentieth. Indeed, the timid and faltering attempts to mount a Philadelphia Bicentennial in 1976 seem to be largely the result of the consciousness of the failure of the city to recover from the forces that so powerfully surrounded the bemused celebrants of the Centennial of 1876.

NOTES

1. Alexis de Tocqueville, *Democracy in America*, Richard D. Heffner, ed. (New York: New American Library, 1964), pp. 189–91, 254–55, 296–313.
2. Russell Blaine Nye, *The Cultural Life of the New Nation, 1776–1830* (New York: Harper and Row, 1963), pp. 3–54.
3. Carl Bridenbaugh, *Cities in Revolt* (New York: Alfred A. Knopf, 1965), p. 248.
4. The first essay in this volume by John Alexander emphasizes this point, as do Gordon Wood, *The Creation of the American Revolution, 1776–1787* (Chapel Hill: University of North Carolina Press, 1969) and Michael Kammen, *People of Paradox* (New York: Knopf, 1972).
5. J. L. Vansant, ed., *The Royal Road to Wealth: An Illustrated History of the Successful Business Houses of Philadelphia* (Philadelphia: Samuel Long, 1869), passim; *Diary of the Japanese Visit to Philadelphia in 1872* (Philadelphia: Ashmead, Printer, 1872), pp. 75–79.
6. Such guides as *Magee's Illustrated Guide of Philadelphia and the Centennial Exhibition* (Philadelphia: Richard Magee and Son, 1876) portray this physical development.
7. Francis A. Walker, *A Compendium of the Ninth Census* (Washington, D.C.: Government Printing Office, 1872), p. 543. Labor force figures appear on p. 619.
8. E. Digby Baltzell, *Philadelphia Gentlemen: The Making of a National Upper Class* (Glencoe, Illinois: The Free Press, 1958), pp. 182–91.
9. Nicholas B. Wainwright, *History of the Philadelphia National Bank* (Philadelphia: The Philadelphia National Bank, 1953), pp. 129–31.
10. Lorin Blodgett, "Building Systems of the Great Cities," a paper read before the Philadelphia Social Science Association, April 5, 1877. In the collection of the Historical Society of Pennsylvania, Philadelphia.

11. Advertisements in the Philadelphia *Public Record* and the *Evening Bulletin* show this trend.
12. *Public Record* (Philadelphia), July 6, 1876.
13. Ibid.
14. Rowland C. Berthoff, *An Unsettled People: Social Order and Disorder in American History* (New York: Harper and Row, 1971), pp. 218–19.
15. John Sutherland, "Housing the Poor in the City of Homes," in Allen F. Davis and Mark Haller, eds., *The Peoples of Philadelphia: A History of Ethnic Groups and Lower-Class Life, 1790-1940* (Philadelphia: Temple University Press, 1973), pp. 175–202; John Sutherland, "The Origins of Philadelphia's Octavia Hill Association: Social Reform in the 'Contented' City," *The Pennsylvania Magazine of History and Biography*, XCIX:1 (January 1975), pp. 20–44.
16. John J. MacFarlane, *History of Early Chestnut Hill* (Philadelphia: City Historical Society, 1927), p. 142; S. F. Hotchkin, *Ancient and Modern Germantown, Mt. Airy and Chestnut Hill* (Philadelphia: P. W. Ziegler, 1889), pp. 442–520.
17. These figures are based on analysis of such maps as the "New Driving Map of Philadelphia and Vicinity" by J. L. Smith of Philadelphia, 1884, "Philadelphia in 1886" by Burk and McFettridge of Philadelphia, 1885, and the many city maps included in guidebooks for 1876. Assuming conservatively fifty homes to a block and twelve residential blocks to a mile on each side of the trackage, these figures result.
18. Davis and Haller, *The Peoples of Philadelphia*, p. 6.
19. *Public Record* (Philadelphia), January 31, 1876.
20. John Daly and Allen Weinberg, *Philadelphia County Political Subdivisions* (Philadelphia: City of Philadelphia, 1966), pp. 98–100.
21. Dennis Clark, "A Pattern of Urban Growth: Residential Development and Church Location in Philadelphia," *Records of the American Catholic Historical Society*, 82:3 (September 1971), pp. 160–70. George Morgan, *Philadelphia: A City of Firsts* (Philadelphia: Historical Publication Society, 1926), p. 258.
22. The *Philadelphia North American*, April 20, 1876.
23. For the riotous first half of the century see Sam Bass Warner, *The Private City: Philadelphia in Three Periods of its Growth* (Philadelphia: University of Pennsylvania Press, 1968), pp. 125–60.
24. Herbert Gutman, "The Workers Search for Power," in H. Wayne Morgan, ed., *The Gilded Age: A Reappraisal* (Syracuse: Syracuse University Press, 1963), pp. 38–68.
25. Thomas Scharf and Thompson Westcott, *History of Philadelphia, 1609-1884*, 3 vols. (Philadelphia: L. H. Everts, 1884), I:838.
26. Ellis P. Oberholtzer, *Philadelphia: A History of the City and Its People*, 3 vols. (Philadelphia: S. J. Clarke, 1921), II:398.
27. Dee Brown, *The Year of the Century: 1876* (New York: Charles Scribner's Sons, 1966), pp. 58–61.
28. The *Philadelphia North American*, March 29, 1876 and April 20, 1876.
29. Russell H. Conwell, *Acres of Diamonds* (Philadelphia: Temple University, 1959), p. 14.
30. The values of this period are explained by John Tipple, "The Robber Baron in the Gilded Age," in Morgan, *The Gilded Age*, pp. 28–29, and John G. Cawelti, *Apostles of the Self-Made Man* (Chicago: University of Chicago Press, 1965), pp. 125–66.
31. Baltzell, *Philadelphia Gentlemen*, pp. 108–26.
32. Ibid., p. 108.
33. Erwin Stanley Bradley, *The Triumph of Militant Republicanism: A Study of Pennsylvania and Presidential Politics, 1860-1872* (Philadelphia: University of Pennsylvania Press, 1964), p. 365; *Gopsill's Philadelphia City Directory* (Philadelphia: James Gopsill, 1876), p. 1663.
34. Data on these institutions is given in Scharf and Westcott, *History of Philadelphia*,

II:1449–91; *Magee's Illustrated Guide,* passim.

35. Edward Strahan (pseudonym of Earl Shinn), *A Century After: Picturesque Glimpses of Philadelphia and Pennsylvania* (Philadelphia: Allen Lane and Scott, 1875), pp. 184–98.
36. Oberholtzer, *Philadelphia: A History of the City,* II, passim.
37. Scharf and Westcott, *History of Philadelphia,* II:1490.
38. The *Philadelphia North American,* February 13, 1876.
39. The *Philadelphia Inquirer,* September 5, 1876.
40. Warner, *Philadelphia: The Private City,* p. 118.
41. Scharf and Westcott, *History of Philadelphia,* I:838. Such problems are listed in chronological order in George Morgan, *Philadelphia: A City of Firsts.*
42. Edward Chase Kirkland, *Industry Comes of Age, 1860–1897* (Chicago: Quadrangle, 1967), pp. 2–10.
43. The *Philadelphia North American,* January 6, 1876.
44. Philip E. Mackey, "Law and Order, 1877: Philadelphia's Response to the Railroad Riots," *Pennsylvania Magazine of History and Biography,* XCVI:2 (April 1972), pp. 183–202.
45. Warner, *The Private City: Philadelphia,* p. 108.
46. The *Philadelphia Inquirer,* August 17, 1876.
47. Oberholtzer, *Philadelphia: A History of the City and Its People,* II:400.
48. Seymour Mandelbaum, *Boss Tweed's New York* (New York: John Wiley, 1965), p. 58.
49. The *Philadelphia North American,* April 5, 1876.
50. Warner, *The Private City,* pp. 85–86.
51. Morgan, *Philadelphia: The City of Firsts,* p. 350.
52. *Historical Development of Local and State Government in the Pen-Jer-Del Region,* Monograph No. 1, Pennsylvania Economy League (Philadelphia: December 1961), pp. 35–40.
53. The *Philadelphia North American,* January 17, 1876.
54. Oberholtzer, *Philadelphia: A History of the City and Its People,* II:402.
55. Ibid., II:402; John Maass, *The Glorious Enterprise: The Centennial Exhibition of 1876* (Watkins Glen, New York: American Life Foundation, 1973), pp. 1–50.
56. Ibid., p. 7.
57. Issues of *Crotzer's Centennial and Journal of the Exposition* are in the Centennial materials collection of the Logan Free Library of Philadelphia.
58. Brown, *The Year of the Century: 1876,* pp. 112–37.
59. Edward Strahan (pseudonym of Earl Shinn), *A Century After,* p. 360.
60. The *Philadelphia North American,* May 15, 1876.
61. The *Philadelphia Inquirer,* July 4, 1876. The Centennial as a manifestation of the American spirit is noted in John Brinkerhoff Jackson, *American Space: The Centennial Years, 1865–1876* (New York: W. W. Norton, 1972), pp. 238–39.
62. The *Philadelphia Inquirer,* July 4, 1876.
63. Maass, *The Glorious Enterprise,* p. 99.
64. Robert Weaver, *The Ethics of Rhetoric* (Chicago: Henry Regnery, 1953), pp. 169–72.
65. Maass, *The Glorious Enterprise,* pp. 92–100.

BICENTENNIAL PHILADELPHIA

A Quaking City

PETER A. McGRATH

Bicentennial Philadelphia (courtesy of the Office of the City
Representative, Philadelphia)

How goes life in Philadelphia two hundred years after it hosted the events that set in motion the break between England and America? On the surface, Philadelphia, like all big cities, seems to be in the process of decay. While it is true that the city does indeed have problems, it is also true that some progress is being made to solve these problems.

The Philadelphia of today is a city of neighborhoods filled with residents who are strongly attached to their particular section of the city. It is also a city of immigrants and their descendants. Every ethnic and racial group calls some part of Philadelphia "home." From a visual perspective, Philadelphia is unique in its diversity.[1] There is the secluded beauty of Fairmount Park's 4,000 acres, the suburban look of the Northeast, the historic charm of Society Hill as well as the poverty reflected in the boarded-up homes in North Philadelphia. But mostly Philadelphia is block after block of red brick row homes.

Philadelphia is a city of traditions as well. Soft pretzels have been sold on downtown street corners for years and every New Year's Day thousands of brightly clad Mummers make the march up Broad Street to the sound of string bands in a parade that lasts from dawn to dusk.

Philadelphia's growth as an industrial center took place during the last half of the nineteenth century and the first quarter of the twentieth century.[2] It was during this period that it became home for immigrants from such countries as Ireland, Germany, Italy, Poland and Russia.[3] The population of the city grew from 408,000 in 1850 to 847,000 in 1880, then in 1920 to 1,823,779.

The years since 1930 show a remarkable stability in terms of the city's population. Total population has hovered around the 2 million level. A major change, however, has been taking place in the city's racial composition. Philadelphia was 11 percent black in 1930 with 219,599 blacks; in 1970 this figure had grown to 33.6 percent and represented 653,791 blacks.

Philadelphia's white population has been moving out to the surrounding suburbs. The extent of this outmigration can be seen in the rate of population growth for each of these suburban counties during the decade of the 1960's. The seven counties grew as follows: Burlington, +67.8 percent;

Bucks, +34.5 percent; Chester, +32.1 percent; Gloucester, +28.1 percent; Montgomery, +20.7 percent; Camden, +16.4 percent; and Delaware, +8.5 percent.

Philadelphia has undergone more than a century and a quarter of social and economic change. After the waves of foreign immigrants began to wane in the 1920's, there came another wave of southern black immigrants. Philadelphia responded slowly and reluctantly to each new group that chose to settle within its boundaries. Eventually, however, each group has participated with varying degrees of success in the life of the city.

Philadelphia, of course, has changed a great deal since the Revolution. This analysis will seek to discover whether the city still reflects the ideals and values of the American Revolution in light of the changes that have occurred. Specifically, three areas of interest will be explored. First, what institutions have developed in Philadelphia and how do they function in the mid-1970's? Next, what problems does the city confront today and what responses have been formulated to cope with these problems? Finally, has progress been made with regard to the quality of life in the city?

PHILADELPHIA'S INSTITUTIONS

Philadelphia life in the mid-1970's exhibits two basic features. One is that a large number of competing public and private institutions are involved in deciding public policy for the city. The other is that the active constituencies of most of these institutions have been shrinking, and the leaders within these institutions have been losing touch with many of those they seek to represent.

Nevertheless, Philadelphia is very much a pluralistic city. No one institution has a monopoly of power in its political life. At the center of the decision-making arena is the city's government.[4] Clustered around this core are a large number of diverse institutions, which serve as avenues of pressure and influence on the city's public affairs. Among these are the news media, religious groups, a wide variety of citywide and neighborhood civic groups, business organizations, academic centers, labor unions and the two major political parties. These institutions for many reasons, however, fail to provide a link to the average Philadelphian.

Much of what is important for Philadelphia in the mid-1970's had its origins twenty-five years earlier, in 1951. In April of that year the voters adopted the Home Rule Charter. Until then, the city had been governed under a series of charters handed down by the Pennsylvania State Legislature. The Home Rule Charter ushered in a new era. Philadelphia was about to have a new government, new leadership and an urban renewal program that would receive national attention.[5]

The Home Rule Charter made noticeable changes in the city's government. It retained the City Council, the mayor and most of the elected administrative offices, frequently referred to as "row offices" because of their nineteenth century location in the row houses that adjoined City Hall. The principal change was the creation of a "strong mayor" form of government. The council was reduced in size, a civil service based on merit selection was inaugurated and limitations were placed on political activity by city employees. Finally, a restriction was placed on the creation of any additional executive departments other than those specified in the charter. The framers of this charter had intended to create a more rational and streamlined city government. Today, it is not clear that this was the result. Problems appear to exist in three areas: council size, mayoral powers and limitations on new departments.

The adoption of this charter, especially with its provision for a reduced council size, continued a century-long trend of centralization of governmental power in City Hall. This trend began in 1854, when the original city of Philadelphia (today's downtown business district) annexed the small townships and boroughs that were part of Philadelphia County.[6] These were flourishing municipalities, which over the next one hundred years lost most of their governmental functions. There are those who argue that much good would come from returning some of the city's governmental functions to the present-day neighborhoods.[7]

The 1951 Home Rule Charter was the third reduction of the council's size in the twentieth century. As a result, city government drifted further away from the average citizen. This trend toward a smaller council size and a corresponding increase in the ratio of council members to citizens is clearly shown by the contrast between 1910, when 1,549,000 residents had 145 council members (a ratio of 1 to 10,682), and 1974, when 1,950,098 residents had 17 council members (a ratio of 1 to 114,711).

The net effect of this shift has been to make effective communication between citizen and government much more difficult. The council member's time must be shared with more people, and thus constituent problems must receive proportionately less attention. There are ten times the number of citizens competing for a council member's time now as there were in 1910.

City life is also much different now than it was in 1910. A communications revolution during the past twenty years has made television the chief source of political information for the average citizen. Yet television stations in Philadelphia can seldom devote time to coverage of the local council member. There is some evidence that Philadelphians are indeed frustrated in their relationship not only with the City Council but also with other local government agencies.

A recent survey of citizen attitudes toward government found that 72.6 percent of those interviewed thought they should have more direct control over the City Council than they do at present. A like number felt the same way about the mayor and the school district.[8]

A second problem may be that there are insufficient checks and balances with respect to the powers now given to the mayor. The Charter writers in 1951 wanted to correct some of the administrative problems that had arisen because of the lack of concentrated responsibility, power and accountability in one elected official. Their solution was a strong mayor.

Most critics would agree that the concept worked well under the first three mayors. Mayor Joseph Clark, followed by Richardson Dilworth, launched the rebirth of the city's historic and commercial areas. Despite numerous political battles, the rebuilding continued under Mayor James H. J. Tate and the city greatly increased its share of federal funding.

In 1971, at a time of great national as well as local increases in crime and racial polarization, the voters elected as mayor their police commissioner, Frank L. Rizzo. During his term, the strong mayor concept would be tested severely. Doubts were raised as to whether it was an outmoded concept. One critic, John Guinther, has asked:

Should one man, whatever his capacities, nearly limitlessly speak for and guide a City of two million people, at the same time directly affecting by his actions the lives of another million or so living in the megalopolis of which Philadelphia is the hub?[9]

Mayor Rizzo's supporters, and there are many, would undoubtedly answer yes. They have continued to support him despite what some consider to be improper behavior. Criticism of the mayor has focused on the following points:

—On Mayor Rizzo's orders, the Philadelphia Police Department arrested a group of peaceful demonstrators at Independence Hall, despite the fact that the Philadelphia District Attorney's Office had ruled that the demonstration was legal. The arrests took place during an October 1972 visit of then-

President Richard M. Nixon, who was in Philadelphia for the signing of the Revenue Sharing Act.

—Local newspapers revealed that the mayor created a special thirty-three-man squad to spy on his political enemies.

—The mayor was in the process of having a $400,000 house built, until the local newspapers questioned his ability to pay for it with only his salary.

—The mayor, and deputy Mayor Philip Carroll, failed to pass a polygraph test to determine whether a bribe had been offered to the local Democratic chairman, Peter J. Camiel.

Supporters of the mayor would argue that much of this is political back-biting and that the mayor's positive actions far outweigh these negative charges. How seriously Philadelphians take these criticisms will be determined during 1975, when Mayor Rizzo stands for reelection. One thing is clear, however, there is no easy answer to the dilemma of whether to have a "strong" or "weak" mayor.

A third problem presents itself in the way Philadelphia's government is limited by the charter. In order to prevent abuses found in the past, the charter placed a firm limit on the number of city departments and boards. New urban needs as well as federal funding responses have made this limitation obsolete. Under the current charter the city must add any new programs to existing departments or boards. Revenue sharing, however, is now transferring to local governments many of the social and economic programs previously carried out by the federal government. Not being able to establish the appropriate departments to coordinate these new approaches puts Philadelphia at a disadvantage. This was recognized by a commission recently convened to review and recommend amendments to the charter.[10]

These problems, however, were not intentionally created by the 1951 charter writers. As an institution, Philadelphia government was forced to make certain trade-offs. The size of City Council was reduced, not to remove its members from the people but to make it more efficient and less likely to pass "pork barrel" legislation. A strong mayor was created not to give any one man too much power, but to remedy a situation in which a mayor did not have enough power. Nor did those who wrote the charter fail to create sufficient checks and balances. The evidence may indeed point to the opposite conclusion with respect to the limitations placed on the creation of new departments.

The city's political life for the past 125 years has been dominated by the existence of a strong political organization operating throughout most parts of the city.[11] Prior to 1951 this organization had been primarily in the hands of the Republican party. With one exception, a Democratic victory in the 1933 district attorney and city controller races, the Republicans won every local election from 1883 to 1951.[12] Since reform Mayor Joseph S. Clark's victory in 1951, the Democrats have won every local election, except 1953, 1965 and 1969.[13]

In the mid-1970's, Philadelphia's politics is primarily a battle for control of the Democratic party. On the fringe of this activity are the city's other political institutions: the quasi-political parties, the news media and civic groups. As will be seen, even further removed are the voters.

In terms of power, the most important political institutions are the political parties. They decide who will be nominated and elected and thus who will have the authority to govern. Four characteristics have come to describe the nature of the city's two major political parties: (1) they are well organized; (2) they control almost every aspect of the election process; (3) the Republican party has lost considerable strength; and (4) as clearly the majority party, the Democratic party has become a battleground for factional disputes.

The degree of political organization in Philadelphia is remarkably high. Both parties, the Democrats more so than the Republicans, maintain a standing political army. The city is divided into sixty-nine wards and each ward is further divided into an average of about twenty-five divisions. Approximately 500 to 600 voters live in each division. Every four years, in the spring primary, both parties elect two committee persons in each division who in turn select a leader in each ward. Of all the institutions and agencies in the city, probably the one closest to the average citizen is the committee person.

This role has been criticized by reformers, and it is often stated that the job of getting out the vote has been replaced by television. Yet it is still the committee person to whom many Philadelphians turn when the bureaucratic agencies of government fail to respond. For many, the committee person still remains the source of information and opinion. This person is still the "poor man's lawyer" and often the sole remaining link within the neighborhood to the impersonal confusing world "downtown."

The second characteristic of Philadelphia's political parties is that they are able to translate their organizational strength into primary election victories. Because of the almost complete lack of political activity outside the formal party organizations, few independent Democrats or Republicans ever win their party's nomination. There is no inexpensive way for most independent candidates to become known to the voters in such an expensive media market as Philadelphia. Nor are there many rewards available that the independent can use to motivate and organize a political force equal to that of the political party. Political leaders in Philadelphia have thus all been selected through the endorsement process of the two major political parties. Most elected officials first serve as ward leaders and then use this position as a base of power to win endorsement from the party.

The third important feature with regard to Philadelphia's political parties is the decline of the Republican party. Republican strength in the city has been on the decline since the 1951 win by the Democrats, but in recent years it has fallen to new levels. Democrats can now carry Philadelphia for national and statewide candidates regardless of political trends outside the city. In 1972, for example, George McGovern won Philadelphia by 90,000 votes. Most other elective offices are also won by the Democrats. The following data shows that Philadelphia has become a one-party town. As of January 1, 1975, offices held by the parties are shown in Table 1.

TABLE 1
PARTY DISTRIBUTION OF OFFICES

Office	Republicans	Democrats
Congressional Seats	0	4
State Senate Seats	1	8
State House Seats	4	30
Mayor	0	1
City Council	3	14
City "Row Offices"	1	7
Local Judges Elected in November 1973	0	44

Source: Calculated from the *Bulletin Almanac*, 1974.

The G.O.P., as the minority party, is guaranteed by law two seats on the council and one of the county commissioner seats. The extent of the decline of the Republican party was shown in 1973, when two relatively unknown Democratic candidates, F. Emmett Fitzpatrick, Jr. and William Klenk, upset two of the strongest Republican vote getters, incumbent District Attorney Arlen Specter and incumbent City Controller Tom Gola. Republican judicial losses in 1973 were also overwhelming. Out of the forty-four contested judgeships up for election, the party was not able to win a single one.

There was a point in the mid-1960's when the percentage of voters registered Republican began to climb. Between 1965 and 1970 Republican registration went from 36.6 percent to 39.1 percent. From 1970 onward, however, the decrease in Republican registration has been rapid, as Table 2 indicates.

This trend toward a Democratic-dominated political system has been accompanied by the increasing tendency toward factional politics among the Democrats. The major political contest during 1974 in Philadelphia was for control of the chairmanship of the party, with Peter J. Camiel winning reelection over a Rizzo-backed candidate. This factional fight has carried over into the 1975 mayoral election, with State Senator Louis G. Hill endorsed by the Democrats to run against Mayor Rizzo for the party's nomination. Factional politics is a likely outcome when one party dominates the political system, and it is likely to continue in Philadelphia for some time.

TABLE 2
PARTY REGISTRATIONS 1969–1974

Year	Percent Registered Republican	Percent Registered Democratic
1969	39.0	58.7
1970	39.1	58.5
1971	35.2	62.1
1972	33.6	63.5
1973	32.9	64.2
1974	30.7	66.6

Source: Calculated from *Annual Report of the Registration Commission for the City of Philadelphia*, 1969–74.

Beyond the inter- and intraparty feuding, but very much involved in the city's political life, are the quasi-political parties, the news media and the civic groups. For the most part, these groups respond to rather than initiate public policy, although on some occasions they have a great influence on the direction that public policy takes.

Quasi-political parties are those groups which actively engage in partisan political activities but do not run their own candidates and do not appear as political parties on the ballot. However, they frequently endorse candidates for office and donate time and/or funds to help such candidates win election.

In Philadelphia, there are numerous groups that could be classified as quasi-parties. The most powerful of these groups is the local COPE chapter, the political arm of the AFL–CIO, and other affiliated labor groups. Normally, COPE gears up to provide candidates with funds and election day workers. These workers usually augment the existing Democratic organization in helping to get out the vote. Most observers credit labor with helping to produce the 1973 Democratic sweep.

Other quasi-political parties are also active, but they exert much less influence than does labor. This category would include such groups as the Americans for Democratic Action, the Central City Reform Democrats, the Black Political Forum, the New Democratic Coalition and the Women's Political Caucus. Their chief aim tends to be political reform. The membership of these groups comes from middle and upper middle income white collar and professional groups. Geographically, their membership is drawn from center city, the neighborhood near the University of Pennsylvania and from the neighborhoods of Germantown, Mount Airy and Chestnut Hill to the northwest.

These groups have little influence on the average Philadelphian voter. They do serve a useful purpose, however, in that they provide an avenue of access to the political process for individuals who do not feel comfortable working within one of the two major parties. This lack of a broad-based political membership has made it difficult for these groups to have much of an impact on the election process from a citywide point of view. They are able, however, to influence the outcome of some contests in areas where their members live. For example, the Americans for Democratic Action recently directed its efforts in an unsuccessful but close recall election campaign against a city council member. This same group has also become somewhat of a gadfly to the Rizzo administration and has filed legal suits charging political use of federal job funds.

Another major force outside the realm of the political parties is the news media. Philadelphia has three major television stations, two news-oriented AM radio stations, three daily newspapers and a monthly magazine. While the electronic news media have been content to report the news as it occurs, the print media have moved into the area of investigative journalism. Leading this trend have been the *Philadelphia Inquirer* and *Philadelphia Magazine*.

The *Inquirer,* until 1969, was owned by Walter Annenberg.[14] In that year, when Annenberg was appointed by President Nixon as U.S. Ambassador to the Court of St. James, he sold the paper to the Knight Newspapers. In the years since, the *Inquirer* and the *Daily News,* as well as the *Bulletin* to a lesser extent, have become active combatants in the city's political process. The success of the *Washington Post's* Woodward and Bernstein with their Watergate stories has probably set off a trend toward investigative journalism that will continue in Philadelphia for quite some time. The news media has indeed become a participant in the city's political life, and not without criticism.[15]

The last major political force in the city are the civic groups. These are generally nonpartisan, privately sponsored groups, which seek to influence public policy. Their constituencies tend to be limited and their major impact comes through their role as "watchdogs."

In many ways they are similar to the quasi-political parties. The major difference is that the civic groups do not become involved in direct political activity. They are, however, a route of access to government for those who lack either the time or the inclination to become involved in partisan political activity. Very often these agencies serve as a vehicle for the business and financial community to take part in the city's affairs.

Philadelphia has a wide diversity of groups, each with its own interests and constituency. Some groups, such as the Chamber of Commerce and the Old Philadelphia Development Corporation, are oriented toward the economic development of the city. Others have emerged at a time of crisis in the city. The Greater Philadelphia Movement was started in 1948 at a time when Philadelphia was in need of political and economic renewal. The Urban Coalition was created in response to the unmet needs of the inner city. Some groups focus on a special area of need: The Fellowship Commission on human relations, the Citizens Crime Commission on law enforcement, the Committee of Seventy on the election process, the Philadelphia Council for Community Advancement and the Housing Association of Delaware Valley on housing, the Pennsylvania Economy League on local government administration and research, the Citizens Committee on Public Education on schools, and the Jaycees, the United Fund and the Health and Welfare Council on human needs. Many more exist on a citywide basis and an even greater number are active in the various neighborhoods.

These civic groups add to the quality of Philadelphia's life in varying ways. To a large extent their effectiveness depends on their ability to establish informal lines of communication with those in political office. At times these groups have been able to do business with the politicians over lunch, but more recently many of them have had to depend on the news release to communicate with City Hall. Their existence in such numbers is further evidence of the pluralism of the city. There is a relative lack of wide participatory memberships among these groups and, while there is a pluralism present in Philadelphia, it is a pluralism of competing elites.

The bottom line in politics is the voters. The institutions of politics must inevitably rest upon the consent of the governed. Without widespread voter support there is no legitimacy and, over the long run, government may continue to exist without the voter, but it does not govern in the true sense of the word. Much of what we have come to call government is really based upon the trust and support supplied by the citizens. There is, therefore, some disturbing evidence beginning to appear in the voting statistics for Philadelphia.

One statistic that should be of great concern deals with the number of citizens of voting age who are registered to vote. More than one in every four adult Philadelphians is not registered to vote, and only 73 percent of the city's population over eighteen years old is registered.

The percent of eligible voters who actually do vote has been declining. The voter turnout in each type of election is shown in Table 3 for the last twelve years.

TABLE 3
VOTER TURNOUT, 1963–1974

Election for	Year	Percent Voting	Year	Percent Voting	Year	Percent Voting	Percent Difference
President	1964	85.8	1968	84.0	1972	76.7	– 9.1
Dist. Attorney	1965	62.2	1969	61.8	1973	44.4	– 17.8
Governor	1966	73.1	1970	68.1	1974	60.1	– 13.0
Mayor	1963	74.9	1967	75.5	1971	76.6	+ 1.7

Source: Calculated from *Annual Report of the Registration Commission for the City of Philadelphia, 1963–1974.*

In three of the four types of elections, the percentage of Philadelphians who vote has been declining. Only in the elections for mayor has there been an increase, and this has been only 1.7 percent. These statistics are actually part of a long-run downward trend, both for Philadelphia and the nation. For example, the Philadelphia voter turnout for governor has been as high as 93 percent in 1930 and 1934.

Voter turnout is even lower for offices at the bottom of the ticket and even lower yet in primary elections. Turnout in primaries is often only 30–35 percent. In effect, decisions as to which candidates will be elected to office are made by a very small number of people. Consider the following statistics: In a hotly contested and well-publicized primary for mayor in 1971, Frank Rizzo received 176,621 votes (49.9 percent of the votes cast) to win the Democratic party nomination over two other candidates. When Rizzo's vote total is computed on the basis of other voter and population totals, the results show that he was nominated by only a fraction of the total adult population. In the 1971 primary election, Rizzo received 49.9 percent of the votes cast but only 29.4 percent of the Democratic votes, 18.3 percent of the votes of those registered and 13.8 percent of the votes of the adult population. This shows the dramatic lack of citizen participation in the candidate selection process. The trend is growing worse, not better.

Another disturbing statistic deals with the number of blacks who are registering to vote.[16] Despite the fact that there has been an increase in the city's black population during the past eight years, there has not been much of an increase in the total number of blacks who are registered. A comparison of the three most recent gubernatorial elections shows virtually no change during the last eight years. In 1966 there were 264,459 blacks registered to vote. In 1970 there were 256,907, and in 1974 the total was 267,328.

In all, about 63 percent of the adult black population is registered to vote. Despite the fact that blacks now make up 35 percent of the city's population, black registration as a percent of total registration is only 28.7 percent. In fact, black registration as a percent of the total has declined slightly (0.1 percent) between 1973 and 1974.

The evidence would seem to indicate that Philadelphians in general, and blacks in particular, are slowly withdrawing from the political process. What is the cause? Why have the city's institutions failed to generate the necessary voter support? It may be that the problems of the city have grown too large and, since no solutions are being found, the citizen has decided to break his social and political contract.

There may be some cynics who would argue that Philadelphia, in the mid-1970's, merely confirms the beliefs held by the Founding Fathers, who basically distrusted the average voter. When the Constitution was originally written, it provided for very little direct voter control over government at the national level. Men such as Hamilton warned of "mobocracy" and gave the voters only one office, the House of Representatives, for which they could vote directly.

On the other hand, the diverse number of competing institutions in Philadelphia today would have pleased the Founding Fathers. They feared the concentration of power and so they would admire the pluralism within the community. The fact, however, that these institutions are dominated by elites and that they lack substantial constituent ties may in the long run be one of the city's greatest weaknesses.

Our society, perhaps, has become too centralized and too specialized. The demands of industrialization and urbanization forced these changes upon us. We benefited, however, from being centralized and specialized. The twentieth century city initially meant greater efficiency and cultural diversity.

Yet the fact remains that there are Philadelphians today who have been cut off, or have cut themselves off, from the political life of the city because of the structural and institutional forces characteristic of a big city.

Political participation for some became impossible because of the lack of time; for others it was the easy way out. Some, however, were never aware that a choice was possible. During the past 125 years, Philadelphia has grown from a cluster of small and scattered townships and boroughs to a complex industrial and commercial center, and this has meant a drastic change in the city's institutions and political system.

Philadelphia has grown so large and complex that politics, like most other things, has been left to the specialist, the party activist, the reformer, the journalist or the civic leader. The average Philadelphian has very little chance of coming into direct contact with the city's elected officials and other key decision-makers. The evening news on television can only treat the day's public policy questions superficially. And even when it attempts a more in-depth review, there is little interest shown by the average citizen. Philadelphia, however, cannot afford to lose the broad base of citizen interest and support that is fundamental to its survival as a community.

Another reason for the decline in citizen participation may be the numerous problems of urban life, which appear to have worsened over the years. As each year passes without solutions being found, citizen confidence in the city's institutions is further destroyed. These problems have become so complex that only the experts have the background to understand them. In time, they may become so pervasive as to threaten our capacity to act. If this happens, these problems will have destroyed the city's will to survive. In increasing numbers, if voting statistics are any guide, the average Philadelphian may no longer feel that his efforts as an individual make any difference. The key to this lack of citizen confidence may indeed lie with the city's problems.

PHILADELPHIA'S PROBLEMS

Philadelphia at the time of the country's 200th anniversary faces the same problems other big cities face. It must cope with a rising crime rate, a housing stock that continues to age and deteriorate and a job base that is declining and shifting beyond its borders to the suburbs. This list of problems also includes schools that often do not educate and a local tax base that evaporates yearly. In many ways, Philadelphia is a city that is overripe. It is suffering from an overdose of 125 years of industrialization, immigration and urbanization. These three forces, more than anything else, are responsible for conditions in Philadelphia today.

No other problem has drawn more attention in Philadelphia than the rising level of crime. It was Philadelphia's fear of crime that was a major factor in the election of former Police Commissioner Frank Rizzo as mayor. The extent of this increase can be seen in the crime statistics as reported by the Philadelphia Police Department.[17] In 1967, there were 30,371 reported serious crimes; in 1972, there were 75,268. This means that the number of serious crimes reported in Philadelphia went up by nearly 150 percent in just five years.

Table 4 indicating the different types of reported crime shows that the largest increases occurred in three categories: larceny, robbery and auto theft.

TABLE 4
SELECTED TYPES OF REPORTED CRIMES

	1967 Actual Cases	1972 Actual Cases	Percentage Increase
Largest			
Larceny	4,024	22,732	+ 465
Robbery	2,919	9,710	+ 233
Auto Theft	6,876	16,040	+ 137
Moderate			
Murder	234	413	+ 76
Burglary	12,482	21,182	+ 70
Smallest			
Aggravated Assault	3,378	4,603	+ 36
Rape	458	588	+ 28

The general causes for these increases are complex and have been the subject of much research and debate.[18] Two important factors appear to have been associated with the rise in crime. One has been the great increase in the use of hard drugs. The other has been the large increase in the number of fifteen- to twenty-five-year-olds in Philadelphia's population, an age bracket that commits a large percentage of all crimes. These are the maturing "babies" born during the postwar "baby boom." More crimes are committed now because there are more people at an age to commit them.

The consequences of this increase in crime have been devastating to the life of the city. People's fears about crime have caused them to fear the city.

Retail businessmen have relocated in safer neighborhoods, often outside the city limits. When this happens, the city loses a source of tax revenue and a neighborhood loses a vital service, such as a drugstore or a corner grocery store. Large industry has left the city (and sometimes the region) because of the lower tax rates, the availability of land and the relative safety from crime to be found in the suburbs. When such firms move out, the city loses a taxpayer, and many in the work force may decide to follow their employers and also move out. Because of the fear of crime, many city residents no longer shop in downtown Philadelphia and instead drive to the suburban malls. Finally, fear of crime within the neighborhood has pushed those residents who could afford it to move beyond the city's borders.

The increase in crime has also placed additional demands on the city's resources. During recent years there has been an increase in the number of persons arrested. Arrests for serious crime in Philadelphia jumped from 14,276 to 21,463, or 50 percent, from 1967 to 1972. Thus, an added burden has been placed on law enforcement agencies. One indication of this is the increase in the size of the police department, which grew 23 percent in this period, from 8,599 to 10,612 in total personnel.

Critics have argued that emphasis on more and better-equipped police is not the answer to the crime problem.[19] So far, there does not appear to be an answer. One optimistic note, however, is that because of the declining birth rate, Philadelphia can expect to have fewer people who are at an age to commit crimes.

In one way or another, most of Philadelphia's problems are related to crime. As long as this problem remains intractable, the city's other problems will also be difficult to overcome.

Because of Philadelphia's age, many of its housing units have begun to deteriorate and in some cases have been abandoned. A look at the statistics presents a rather bleak but improving picture. Estimates vary on the number of abandoned housing units, but the 1970 Census puts the number of abandoned units at 31,245. This represents a decline of more than 2,000 units from 1960, which is slightly more than a 6 percent decrease.[20]

There were other gains in housing made during the decade of the 1960's, as Table 5 shows.

During the 1960's the total number of housing units increased by 3.8 percent. At the same time, the number of housing units without plumbing decreased significantly, as did the total number of overcrowded units. The fact remains, however, that 40,647 of the city's housing units are overcrowded, which represents 6 percent of the total housing stock. There is also the problem of the 31,000 abandoned units within the city.

The effect of bad housing is felt by those who must live in it as well as by those who live near it. The existence of abandoned and overcrowded housing destroys the confidence of those who still live in the neighborhood and leads to a decline in property values. This leads to further abandonment if rents fail to rise with the cost of carrying the property. Landlords cease to provide maintenance, and soon another property is abandoned as not worth the cost of upkeep. During the 1960's, property values fell in much of North Philadelphia and in some parts of West Philadelphia, Germantown and Kensington.

TABLE 5
HOUSING GAINS DURING 1960's

	1960	1970	Percent Change
Total Housing Units	649,036	673,390	+ 3.8
Total Units Lacking Plumbing Facilities	26,604	15,615	– 41.3
Overcrowded Housing Units	45,209	40,647	– 10.1

Source: *Housing Characteristics, 1960 and 1970, For Philadelphia Census Tracts* (Philadelphia, Pa.: Philadelphia City Planning Commission, 1972).

To halt the further spread of abandonment, the city introduced an innovative effort in 1973 known as the Urban Homesteading Program.[21] Under this program, vacant homes are sold by the city to qualified buyers for one dollar. The purchaser must agree to rehabilitate and live in the house for five years. The program aims at reclaiming between 200 and 300 properties per year. The bulk of the housing problem is an income problem and will not be solved until real incomes increase throughout the city.

As a matter of fact, the entire housing problem is very much an income problem. For example, the recent increase in the cost of housing has priced many Philadelphians out of the housing market. The city has in the past tried any number of housing programs, but these are only band-aids. In the long run, the solution to the housing problem is an across-the-board rise in the level of real income. The city by itself, however, will never be in a position to solve the housing problem, in the same way that it cannot solve the crime problem. As a result, there is always a great deal of frustration when the city fails to live up to expectations.

A recent work by Jane Jacobs argues that people came to live in cities because this is where there was work. The addition of new people leads to more work, which in turn leads to more people. Cities, according to Jacobs, are economic organs, which can be either growing or dying, depending on the level and type of economic activity (work) they are able to sustain.[22] For Philadelphia, there is evidence that the city is in a period of rapid economic change. Some of the evidence is encouraging; some of the other evidence, however, is gloomy. First, the bad news.

Philadelphia has been losing jobs while employment opportunities have been growing in the suburbs. The change, which occurred during the 1960's, meant that the jobs in the city fell by 11.2 percent (869,748 in 1960 to 772,324 in 1970), while suburban jobs rose by 22.5 percent (592,784 to 726,202).

Recent data from the U.S. Department of Labor's Bureau of Labor Statistics shows a continuation of this trend. Between 1971 and October 1974, the city lost another 19,000 jobs. The most significant change during this period was the loss of manufacturing employment. In the last three years, the city has lost 45,200 blue collar jobs. This represents 9.1 percent of the city's blue collar employment.

The loss of jobs in this area has been partially offset by an increase in other types of jobs. One area that has increased is government employment. During the 1960's, the increase was from 90,445 in 1960 to 129,445 in 1970, a rise of 43 percent.

Increases in government employment have been criticized as wasteful of the taxpayer's money. Without them, however, Philadelphia would have been much harder hit by the loss of jobs that did occur. On the other hand, the increased employment in the city's government meant an increase in local taxes, and this may have been responsible for the job loss in the first place. The number of city employees increased by 37.7 percent between 1950 and 1970, despite the fact that the city's population fell by 6.1 percent.

Services are Philadelphia's greatest growth area. Substantial increases have occurred during the past ten years in medical and health care, insurance, banking and higher education. If this trend away from manufacturing to services continues at the same rate for the next ten years, Philadelphia will be a drastically different city by the mid-1980's.

Another bright spot is the growth in the city's port activities. The total number of tons handled by the port has been steadily increasing. During the ten-year period 1963–1972, the increase in total tons handled through the port was 27 percent.[23]

Philadelphia has been working hard to find solutions to its economic problems. One innovative project is the Philadelphia Garment Board.[24] This is a cooperative venture linking business, labor and government in an attempt to protect the textile industry from a further loss of jobs. Another major development is "Franklin Town," a commercial and residential center being built in the northwest quadrant of center city. There is also the Market Street East Project, which aims at the redevelopment of the Market Street retail area from the Delaware River to City Hall. At the foot of Market Street along the Delaware River will be Penn's Landing, a multi-use development project.

These large semipublic development projects should produce more tax revenues for the city and more jobs for its residents. They should also further stimulate the private redevelopment that has been underway since the 1950's. One effect of these initial redevelopment efforts is the large number of middle and upper middle income residents who have begun to resettle in the neighborhoods clustering around the downtown business district. Real median family income increased in these areas by 82 percent during the period 1960-1970. This was an increase of more than two and one-half times that for the rest of the city.

Not everyone in Philadelphia supports this approach to economic development. Some opposition has been based on the charge that development has occurred at the expense of current residents, primarily low-income blacks.[25] Others, such as the Council of City-wide Community Organizations, argue that the funds should be spent on neighborhood development rather than in the downtown business district.[26]

The choice is a difficult one. The city should be home for both rich and poor, and the latter should not be forced to suffer the trauma of relocating from an area that had been home for a lifetime. In addition, neighborhood development is also a worthwhile goal. The challenge is to strike a balance between these goals and the absolutely essential goal of attracting business, jobs and persons with higher incomes back to the city. Without these projects, the city in the long run would be unable to continue to pay its bills.

Philadelphia's school system has been a source of continual controversy in recent years. The controversies have included student demonstrations, teacher strikes, desegregation policies, budget deficits and accusations that the schools have failed to provide a quality education for a majority of their pupils.

In addition, there has been ongoing political feud between the School Board, which is appointed by the mayor, and the current school superintendent, Matthew Costanzo. The previous school superintendent, Mark Shedd, was also the center of political controversy. In fact one of Mayor Rizzo's campaign pledges during his race for mayor in 1971 was to fire Mark Shedd. Within weeks of the election, Shedd's contract was bought out by the School Board.[27]

One of the most potentially explosive problems, which has yet to be resolved, is the question of school desegregation. At the time of this writing, the School Board is under a court order to develop an acceptable desegregation plan for Philadelphia's school system.

The basic cause of the problem lies in Philadelphia's demographic patterns. White students make up only 34.1 percent of the public school enrollment. Most of these students live in the solidly white neighborhoods of the Northeast, while most of the black students live in the solidly black neighborhoods of North and West Philadelphia. Philadelphia's housing patterns make desegregation of the schools virtually impossible without substantial two-way busing.

The court order to desegregate has set up a confrontation of dramatic proportions. Most evidence indicates that there is strong opposition to the concept of busing. A survey conducted in November 1974 showed little support for busing. Only 16 percent of those interviewed were in favor of it and 72 percent were opposed, with 18 percent of all respondents saying they would break the law to oppose it.[28]

Another facet to the school problem is financial. Each year the school budget goes up more than the previous year. One reason for the problem is that school enrollments have been climbing while the total city population has been declining. In 1950 enrollment was 209,956 and population was 2,071,605. In 1960 it was 236,209 out of 2,002,512 people, and in 1970 it was 291,100 out of 1,948,609 people. Thus, school enrollment grew from 10.1 percent in 1950 to 14.9 percent in 1970. Philadelphia thus has had to educate more children but has had fewer taxpayers available to pay the bills. Declining birth rates should help to ease this problem from the mid-1970's onward.

Critics have raised the question of whether the public schools are providing a quality education. Most evidence shows that Philadelphia students fall below the average for the rest of the nation in national reading tests. Table 6 shows the results obtained for the California Achievement Test given to senior high school students in May 1974.

Discipline and drop-outs are also a problem in the school system. In the 1972–73 school year, there was a total of 1,381 serious school incidents, which would include assaults, alcohol and drug use, robbery, racial disturbances, gang fights and weapons possession.[29] The high school drop-out rate is also significant. In 1973, a total of 9,444 high school students left school. This represents 14.2 percent of all enrolled high school students, the highest of all previous years.[30]

TABLE 6
SENIOR HIGH SCHOOL READING SCORES

| | *Percentage of Pupils* | | | |
	Below 16th Percentile	*16 to 49th Percentile*	*50 to 84th Percentile*	*Above 84th Percentile*
National Norm	15	34	35	16
City Norm	29	38	24	9

Source: Philadelphia *Inquirer,* December 18, 1974, p. 1–B.

There have been efforts, however, to find solutions to these problems. During the past several years, seventy-five alternative educational programs have been developed to offer students a less formal, more personalized approach. One of these is the nationally recognized Parkway School, a "school without walls," which utilizes the city's public and cultural institutions as its classrooms.

Despite these efforts, however, the schools appear to be unable to function as they should. Almost everything has been tried. These innovative programs have been accompanied by a doubling expenditure per pupil from 1966 to 1974 and a 30 percent increase in the number of educational staff per thousand pupils since 1964.[31] Citizens and parents have become frustrated by the fact there seems to be an inverse relationship between improvements in the school system and the amount of tax money being spent. The problem is that cause and effect in education are difficult to identify. The problem is much too complex and, as a result, solutions have been elusive. It may be that much is now expected of the school system over which it, in fact, has little control.

The ability of a city to cope with its problems is directly related to its ability to generate the taxes necessary to fund city services. For Philadelphia, costs have been rising, problems have been growing and the tax base has been shrinking. As a consequence, in the past ten to fifteen years dramatic changes have occurred in the way the city pays its bills.

The bills themselves have risen substantially during the 1960's and early 1970's. Increases in the cost of government and the cost of education from 1962 to 1972 were: In Philadelphia's annual operating budget, $290.6 million to $812.1 million, up 179 percent; in the school district operating budget, $114.7 million to $406 million, up 254 percent; and in the total municipal budget, from $405.3 million to $1,218.1 million, a rise of 201 percent.

Overall, the combined city government and school district budgets have gone up by 201 percent. The largest increase took place in the school budget, with education costs rising by 254 percent in the eleven-year period.

These increases reflect the general inflationary trends in the country as well as the increasing problems confronting the city. A study of Philadelphia by the Federal Reserve Bank showed that the biggest expenditure increases occurred in the areas of employee pensions, health care and law enforcement.[32]

In terms of personnel, the largest increase came in the field of law enforcement. The District Attorney's Office staff rose 72.7 percent; the courts (common pleas and municipal), 49.4 percent; prisons, 37.0 percent; sheriff's office, 30.6 percent; police department, 23.0 percent; and clerk of quarter sessions court, 11.1 percent.

These figures show the effect on government of the large increase in crime during this period. The greatest increases were in government agencies that must respond to crimes already committed. Substantial increases occurred in the number of employees working in the district attorney's office, the courts and the prisons. During the five-year period 1968–1973, the total case load of the Defender Association, a city-funded agency that provides free legal aid to approximately 80 percent of the individuals accused of criminal activity, increased from 24,887 in 1968 to 84,000 in 1973.

The large increase in crime has thus meant a substantial increase in the resources devoted to law enforcement. On the other hand, Table 7 shows that the resources available for other municipal services have been drastically reduced.

Thus, the city has shifted its priorities. Parks and libraries become a luxury in a time of rising crime. Philadelphia finds itself trapped in a frustrating dilemma. Crime is soaring, up 148 percent during the five-year period 1967–1972. This crime has probably contributed to the exodus from the city. By cuttting back on municipal services, the city only adds to the negative impact made by the rising crime rate. The net effect is that there are fewer people to pay taxes.

Consequently, the way the city pays its bills has also changed drastically. In 1962, 31 percent of the city's revenues came from the real estate tax. In 1973, only 14.6 percent of revenues came from this source. This decline has been made up in two ways. To a minor degree, various city wage and income taxes now pay a larger share of the total budget. Because of rising incomes and wages due to inflation, and because the city has been willing to raise the tax rate, the percentage of revenue generated by wage and income taxes has gone up from 28.2 to 33.7.

The most important source of revenue growth, however, has been the federal government. In 1962, Philadelphia received $4.8 million from the federal government. In 1973, the total amount received was $142.4 million. As a percent of the city's total revenues, this represents an increase from 1.6 percent in 1962 to 17.5 percent in 1973.

TABLE 7
PERSONNEL REDUCTIONS FROM 1968 to 1973

City Agency	Percent Decrease in Personnel, 1968–73
Fairmount Park	49.9
City Planning Commission	37.6
Free Library	29.2
Philadelphia General Hospital	20.1
Streets Department	15.4
Commission on Human Relations	12.7
Youth Study Center	9.9
Department of Welfare	6.0
Department of Public Health	5.7
Department of Recreation	2.6

Source: Calculated from data in the *Bulletin Almanac,* 1969 and 1974.

The school district budget has undergone the same type of transformation, except the major new source of support has been the Commonwealth of Pennsylvania as opposed to the federal government. In 1962, real estate taxes paid for 56.8 percent of the school budget, but by 1973 they accounted for only 32.9 percent. State aid grew during this period from 29.9 percent of revenues to 54.7 percent of revenues.

The reasons for the decline of the property tax yield are complex. One obvious reason is the flight of tax-paying residents and businesses to the suburbs. A measure of this decline can be seen in Table 8. Except in two instances, decreases occurred during the past five years in every category of taxable business properties.

Another factor has been at work. During recent years, the city has been losing some of its tax base because of the substantial increase in tax exempt properties, which has increased by 30 percent during the five-year period

1968-1973. More significantly, the percent of tax exempt property value has jumped from 34.8 in 1968 to 40.2 in 1973. An ever-increasing percentage of the city, therefore, is being lost for tax purposes. This land is often converted into classrooms, hospital research laboratories or museums. Ironically, education, health and culture, some of the chief benefits to urban life, also contribute to the city's financial dilemma.

TABLE 8
CHANGE IN REAL ESTATE TAX REVENUE 1968 to 1973

Type of Business Property	Percent Change (1968-73)
Finance Buildings	– 34.1
Public and Commercial Garages	– 16.8
Supermarkets	– 11.9
Dry Cleaning and Laundries	– 10.8
Warehouse, Storage and Loft Buildings	– 7.4
Shops, Factories, Mills and Breweries	– 7.0
Banks, Trusts and Saving Companies	– 4.3
Stores and Business Places	– 2.2
Gasoline Stations	– 1.1
Office Buildings	+ 13.7
Loft and Light Manufacturing	+ 18.3

Source: Calculated from data in the *Bulletin Almanac,* 1969 and 1974.

There is some hope, however, that state and federal funds will continue to flow to the city in sufficient volume to pay its bills. There is a certain justice to this solution. The more the city is called upon to provide services to those beyond its borders, and thus beyond its tax base, the more need there is to shift the burden of paying for these services to as broad a base as possible.

PHILADELPHIA'S PROGRESS AND PROSPECTS

The evidence in the preceding section is that Philadelphia has had to contend with a series of problems that have come to be called the "urban crisis." The tendency of every age, however, is to emphasize the immediate problems and to discount any progress that may have been made. In this section, however, the question to be asked is: Has there been any progress, and if so, what kind? Also, where are we going from here and what of the problems of the future?

One of the key indicators of prosperity in a community is family income. In this category, Philadelphians were definitely better off in 1970 than they were in 1960. Median family income (in 1960 dollars) rose 23.1 percent, from $5,782 to $7,118.

Philadelphia families had a real income gain (after inflation) of $1,336 in yearly income. This was an increase of 23.1 percent and takes into account the offsetting effect of rising prices.

Although income gains were made in Philadelphia during the 1960's, this progress was not as great as the income gains in the surrounding suburbs and in the nation as a whole. Among all the counties in the Philadelphia area, Philadelphia ranks last in terms of real income gains. Table 9 shows the progress made by the surrounding counties during the sixties.

TABLE 9
CHANGE IN REAL INCOME, DURING 1960's

County	Percentage Gain in Real Income
Chester	33.6
Burlington	33.4
Bucks	30.6
Gloucester	27.3
Montgomery	26.9
Camden	24.4
Delaware	23.3
Philadelphia	23.1

Source: *Socio-Economic Characteristics, 1960 and 1970, for Philadelphia Census Tracts*, p. 7.

Philadelphia also lagged behind the income gains made on a national scale. In 1960, median family income for Philadelphia was only $53 below that of the nation. By 1970, Philadelphia median family income was $850 below that of the nation. Put another way, incomes (in actual dollars) grew by 75.4 percent for the nation as a whole in the 1960's, but the rate of median family income growth in Philadelphia was only 62 percent, from $5,782 in 1960 to $9,366 in 1970. In sum, there has been progress, but not to the same extent as in the suburbs and in the rest of the nation. There are some, however, who would argue that this is no progress at all.

Another area where improvement has been made is the number of years of schooling completed. But again, while median education levels went up during the 1960-1970 period, they did not match the increases made nationally. A comparison of Philadelphia with the rest of the nation shows median school years completed in the city were 9.6 in 1960 and 10.9 in 1970, while in the United States the completed years were 10.5 in 1960 and 12.2 in 1970. In 1960, the gap between Philadelphia and the rest of the nation was nine-tenths of a year. This gap had increased by 1970 to 1.3 years.

Despite this failure to move ahead as fast as the rest of the nation, Philadelphia made some remarkable gains. Perhaps the most striking were in the number of Philadelphians who were graduating from high school in 1970 (39.9 percent) and the corresponding number who had never been to high school (33.5 percent). These figures show that a substantial gain of 9.2 percent was made in high school completions in ten years. Philadelphia has a long way to go, however, since about 60 percent of its adult population still has less than a high school education.

At the upper end of the educational scale, progress has been extremely slow. The percentage of Philadelphians with three or more years of college education went up by only 2 percent, from 10.2 percent in 1960 to 12.2 percent in 1970. More rapid progress, however, can be expected in the future, since Philadelphia did not open its Community College until 1965. Since that year, many Philadelphians who could not have afforded a college education have been given this opportunity. Another factor in the slow growth in the percentage of Philadelphians with college experience is the high rate of upward social and economic mobility of individuals who go to college. With degree in hand, they can afford to trade the Philadelphia neighborhood of row houses where they grew up for a home on a quarter-acre in the suburbs.

A major question for a city that is now approximately 35 percent black is how much racial progress has been made. On the positive side, blacks in Philadelphia made significant income gains during the 1960's. Between 1960 and 1970 median black family income increased by 74.1 percent, while that of white families increased by only 63.2 percent. Black incomes are still not equal to white incomes but the gap has been narrowed, while an increase of 4.5 percent in income parity between blacks and whites has been achieved.

Employment opportunities for blacks in Philadelphia improved substantially during the 1960's. The percent of blacks in white collar jobs nearly doubled between 1960 and 1970. Opportunities also improved in skilled job categories, while the percentage of blacks working as laborers declined slightly. Table 10 points out the extent of these employment gains for blacks.

Gains by blacks in the employment area have been matched by gains in the area of education. During the 1960's the percent of blacks with a high school degree went up by 17.1, from 17 to 34.1.

TABLE 10
PERCENT OF JOBS HELD BY BLACKS

Occupation	1960	1970	Percent Change
Total White Collar	11.7	20.3	+ 8.6
Professional and Technical	12.4	18.4	+ 6.0
Managers	7.0	13.5	+ 6.5
Sales Workers	8.3	12.9	+ 4.6
Clerical	14.2	25.2	+ 11.0
Craftsmen	14.6	23.8	+ 9.2
Operatives	29.3	38.1	+ 8.8
Laborers	54.4	53.8	− 0.6

Source: *Socio-Economic Characteristics, 1960 and 1970, for Philadelphia Census Tracts*, p. 23.

At the upper end of the educational scale, black progress was made only slowly, the percent of blacks with one or more years of college increasing from 6.6 in 1960 to only 7.8 in 1970.

Another small indication of progress has been the increase in the number of blacks who owned their own home. During the 1960's this figure increased from 42.9 percent to 47.4 percent. Again, not a great leap forward, but some advancement nevertheless.

Substantial political gains have also been made by Philadelphia's blacks during recent years. Table 11 shows that the most visible gains were in the number of blacks elected to political office.

Black political representation increased by 11.3 percent, while the percent of registered black voters increased by only 4.9 percent. As has been pointed out, however, the number of registered blacks is significantly below the total adult black population. Parity in this area is essential.

Black progress has not occurred in every aspect of Philadelphia life. Two major problems remain unsolved. One is the lack of integration in housing patterns, and the other is the resultant segregation in the school system. There are integrated neighborhoods, such as Mount Airy and Wynnefield, and these appear to be surviving and perhaps flourishing. In fact the number of integrated census tracts, those with between 25 and 75 percent black populations, increased from 15 percent in 1960 to 23 percent in 1970. On the other hand, however, the percent of census tracts with black populations of 75 percent or more has gone up from 11 in 1960 to 18 in 1970.

On the whole, the weight of the evidence is that there has been progress made by blacks in Philadelphia. The city has been a source of opportunity for blacks in income, employment, education, housing and politics. The advancement has been slow to moderate, but the trend line is overwhelming in its upward direction.

TABLE 11
BLACK OFFICE HOLDERS

	1963	1974	Percent Change
Blacks as a Percent of Total Registered Voters	23.8	28.7	+ 4.9
Percent of Elected Offices Held by Blacks	14.1	25.4	+ 11.3
Representation Gap	9.7	3.3	− 6.4

What of the prospects for the city's future? Will the improvements shown here continue, of have they come to an end? Two factors will be important in the short run: the election for mayor in 1975 and the outcome of the court desegregation order. Both of these events have the potential for doing serious damage to the fabric of the community. It appears that Philadelphia is in for events that will test its institutions and its people.

The long-run factors, however, will be more important in determining the direction in which the city is headed. Philadelphia's future will depend on the ability of its institutions (1) to preserve the city's economic life and (2) to reduce crime. The city will prosper if it can rejuvenate itself as an economic entity and, at the same time, eliminate the fact and fear of crime.

A primary condition for a healthy political climate is a sound economic climate, and vice versa. The two century-old values of individual liberty and equality of opportunity will continue to flourish in Philadelphia as long as Philadelphia can flourish economically.

The city must, therefore, continue to be a magnet for commerce, business and employment. From an economic standpoint, it must continue to experience spontaneous bursts of growth from within itself as well as in response to outside stimuli. The city has lost a substantial part of its industrial and manufacturing base, but it has a competitive advantage in supplying services, especially where a central location is important. The rejuvenation process has already begun with such projects as Franklin Town, Penn's Landing and Market Street East. There is much also that has been initiated from beyond the city's borders. There has been a healthy impetus from the federal side in the form of grants and revenue sharing. The city needs a larger tax base to enable it to provide such municipal services as education and police protection, and a continuing growth of jobs to provide a decent and adequate income for those who live in the city.

Any urban strategy must also include as a goal the reduction of crime. Not to do so would be like trying to fill a bathtub without putting in the plug. The problem, however, is that nothing seems to work. On the one hand, much has been written about the correlation between socio-economic environment and crime. At the same time that Philadelphians were making progress in terms of income, education and housing, however, the level of crime was going up dramatically. Likewise, there do not appear to be any quick political solutions to the problem. Philadelphia's "toughest cop," Frank Rizzo, has been either police commissioner or mayor for the last decade, yet crime rates have continued to soar. Until some reduction can be achieved, the future success of Philadelphia must remain in doubt.

As the city moves toward the celebration of the 200th anniversary of the Declaration of Independence, its citizens are distracted by a local unemployment rate that has jumped to 8 percent and threatens to go higher. At the same time, rapid inflation during the past two years has begun to wipe out the income gains made during the 1960's. There is great danger in this. Seymour Martin Lipset has written about the ability of the United States to survive the first troubled decades after the Revolution and the adoption of the Constitution. He points out that America provided a setting in which individual citizens could prosper economically, while it guaranteed individual rights and liberties. Americans, he wrote, accepted our form of government because it worked. It provided a "payoff."[33]

Philadelphia faces this same challenge of survival today. The city must find solutions to the problems of crime and economic decline so as to preserve the fundamental trust that is necessary for the community's institutions to function.

NOTES

1. A recent book on this subject is Richard S. Wurman and John A. Gallery, *Man-Made Philadelphia: A Guide to Its Physical and Cultural Environment* (Cambridge, Mass.: MIT Press, 1972).
2. A useful work on this topic is Sam Bass Warner, Jr., *The Private City: Philadelphia in Three Periods of Its Growth* (Philadelphia: University of Pennsylvania Press, 1968).
3. There is a growing body of material on this topic. Dennis Clark, *The Irish in Philadelphia: Ten Generations of Urban Experience* (Philadelphia: Temple University Press, 1973); Allen F. Davis and Mark H. Haller, eds., *The Peoples of Philadelphia: A History of Ethnic Groups and Lower-Class, 1790-1940* (Philadelphia: Temple University Press, 1973). A rich volume on blacks in Philadelphia written in 1899 and recently reissued is W. E. B. Du Bois, *The Philadelphia Negro: A Social Study* (New York: Schocken, 1967). Two noteworthy works on upper-class Philadelphians are E. Digby Baltzell, *Philadelphia Gentlemen: The Making of a National Upper Class* (New York: The Free Press, 1958) and Nathaniel Burt, *The Perennial Philadelphians: The Anatomy of an American Aristocracy* (Boston: Little, Brown, 1963).
4. The most complete volume on this topic is Edwin Rothman et al, *Philadelphia Government,* 6th ed. (Philadelphia: Pennsylvania Economy League, 1963). A 7th edition is currently in preparation.
5. See Jeanne Lowe, *Cities in a Race with Time: Progress and Poverty in America's Renewing Cities* (New York: Random House, 1967), pp. 313-404; David Rodgers, "Philadelphia: A Planning and Reform Ethos," chapter 3 in *The Management of Big Cities,* pp. 75-104; Kirk Petchek, *The Challenge of Urban Reform* (Philadelphia: Temple University Press, 1973).
6. Milton Kotler, *Neighborhood Government: The Local Foundations of Political Life* (New York: Bobbs-Merrill), pp. 1-13.
7. John Guinther, *The City and the County* (Philadelphia: Philadelphians Who Care, no date), mimeographed, pp. 1-11; Conrad Weiler, *Philadelphia: Neighborhood, Authority, and the Urban Crisis* (New York: Praeger, 1974).
8. C. Weiler, *Philadelphia: Neighborhood, Authority, and the Urban Crisis,* p. 13.
9. John Guinther, *The City and the County,* p. 3.
10. *Report of the City Charter Revision Commission* (Philadelphia: City Charter Revision Commission, 1973), pp. 10-13.
11. One of the best early accounts is James Bryce, *The American Commonwealth,* Vol. II (New York: Macmillan, 1889), see especially chapter LXXXIX, "The Philadelphia Gas Ring," pp. 354-71. Also see, Philip S. Benjamin, "Gentlemen Reformers in the Quaker City, 1870-1912," *Political Science Quarterly,* LXXXV:1 (March 1970), pp. 61-81.
12. For an account of the 1933 Democratic upset, see Irwin F. Greenberg, "Philadelphia Democrats Get a New Deal: The Election of 1933," *The Pennsylvania Magazine of History and Biography,* XCVII:2 (April 1973), pp. 210-32.
13. The following works contain a useful description of Philadelphia politics at various points in the last twenty-five years: James Reichley, *The Art of Government: Reform and Organization Politics in Philadelphia* (New York: The Fund for the Republic, 1959); Robert L. Freedman, *A Report on Politics in Philadelphia* (Cambridge: Joint Center for Urban Studies, 1936); Edward C. Banfield, *Big City Politics* (New York: Random House, 1965), see especially chapter 7, "Philadelphia: Nice While It Lasted," pp. 107-20; Neal R. Pierce, *The Megastates of America: People, Politics, and Power in the Ten Great States* (New York: W. W. Norton, 1972), see especially pp. 262-86.
14. See Gaeton Fonzi, *Annenberg: A Biography of Power* (New York: Weybright and Talley, 1970).

15. For an interesting account of the news media's most recent tilts with local politicians see Mike Mallowe, "In Defense of Emmett Fitzpatrick," *Philadelphia Magazine* (November 1974), p. 108.

16. A useful volume on this topic is Miriam Ershkowitz and Joseph Zikmund, eds., *Black Politics in Philadelphia* (New York: Basic Books, 1973).

17. These statistics may underreport the true level of crime. A recent report from the U.S. Law Enforcement Assistance Agency stated that less than 20 percent of all crimes committed in Philadelphia are actually reported.

18. One of the most comprehensive reviews of this problem is Marvin E. Wolfgang, "Urban Crime," in *The Metropolitan Enigma*, James Q. Wilson, ed. (Cambridge, Mass.: Harvard University Press, 1968), pp. 245–81.

19. See C. Weiler, *Philadelphia: Neighborhood, Authority, and the Urban Crisis*, pp. 179–206.

20. As reported in *Housing Characteristics, 1960 and 1970, For Philadelphia Census Tracts* (Philadelphia: Philadelphia City Planning Commission, 1972), p. 24. There is little agreement on the actual number of abandoned properties. Some estimates by community leaders have put the figure at 40,000. As of 1974, the city's Department of Licenses and Inspections estimates that there are only 26,000 abandoned properties.

21. The most recent and comprehensive description of this program is: Samuel P. Katz, *Urban Homesteading: A Status Report* (Philadelphia: The Philadelphia Partnership, November 1974), pp. 1–19, mimeographed. The driving force behind this program has been City Councilman Joseph Coleman, who first proposed the idea to the Philadelphia City Planning Commission in 1968.

22. Jane Jacobs, *The Economy of Cities* (New York: Random House, 1969).

23. *Bulletin Almanac*, 1974, p. 416.

24. The two individuals most responsible for putting this program together were James Mahoney of the International Ladies Garment Workers Union and James Martin of the Old Philadelphia Development Corporation.

25. See "Blacks Being Pushed Out of Center City?" Philadelphia *Inquirer*, January 7, 1965, p. 1-C.

26. See "Market Street East Opposed," Philadelphia *Evening Bulletin*, December 26, 1974, p. 56.

27. One of the best accounts of the events leading up to this confrontation between Shedd and Rizzo can be found in Peter Binzen, *White Town USA* (New York: Random House, 1970).

28. This survey was conducted by a national polling firm for a local political candidate.

29. Philadelphia *Inquirer*, June 23, 1974, p. 4-B.

30. "Dropout Rate on the Rise Here," Philadelphia *Daily News*, November 5, 1974, p. 4.

31. "Some Facts on Philadelphia School Staffing," *Citizens' Business* (Pennsylvania Economy League), May 25, 1973.

32. William A. Cozzens, "Philadelphia's Budgets: Past, Present, Future," Federal Reserve Bank of Philadelphia, *Business Review* (April 1974), pp. 3–19.

33. Seymour Martin Lipset, *The First New Nation: the United States in Historical and Comparative Perspective* (New York: Basic Books, 1963), p. 45.

PHILADELPHIA 2076

Life in a World of Limits

GRAHAM S. FINNEY

2 0 7 6

Our best early warning systems would suggest that this volume may abruptly end at some point midway through the chapter I have been asked to write. Whether that end is signaled by a bang (nuclear war) or a whimper (no food) is incidental. The Club of Rome, respected ecologists and the simple straight-line projections of many untutored observers all suggest that the future of the planet, much less Philadelphia, is soon slated for calamity unless major societal adjustments are made; that human life and western civilization, much less the revolutionary principles of the American Revolution, are in mortal danger.

The list of impinging forces has become a familiar one, almost wearily recited by the press and from the pulpit. Writers such as Robert Heilbroner and Barry Commoner spell them out in no uncertain terms. What is more distressing, however, is almost daily personal confirmation that such events are in the making. Whether measured in the shrinking Dow-Jones average or in local rates of alcoholism, functional illiteracy, smoking-induced cancer or child abuse, Philadelphians can find ample reason to be apocalyptic in their thinking. Unemployment reaches 8 percent. Gang killings rage unabated in the City of Brotherly Love. The rip-off has become a citywide phenomenon. And rarely a day goes by without a demand for the indictment of a public official or an actual conviction.

In such an atmosphere, concern about abstract principles or imaginative plans to revitalize Philadelphia have lost the place they held in the short-lived renaissance of the 1950's and 1960's, much less in the years surrounding independence. There is, instead, a dominant instinct to survive, to hang on to what one has, especially to one's personal security.

Today, somehow, the American dream, so gloriously articulated in Philadelphia 200 years ago, appears outdated if not naive to many Philadelphians. The staggering scale of government, corporate and other institutions draws into question man's capacity to direct them, to say nothing of using them to meet his individual requirements. The shoe seems on the other foot. We daily ask: Is the city governable?

Many Philadelphians, like many Americans, feel powerless to influence the direction of their nation or city, despite the massive bits of data that rain upon them—down to the scars on leaders' faces and the details of their bank accounts. Unattenuated information leaves us alternatively vexed, numb or rebellious. We suffer from civic neurasthenia: a mental state in which the individual lashes out and then sinks back in fitful slumber, as if to acknowledge the distance between daily life and the awesome strength of external coercions upon the future.

BOARDING A MOVING TRAIN

Against such a setting, to which the writer is not immune, the task of writing about Philadelphia a hundred years from now is approached with great trepidation. It should be an imaginative opportunity, without the need to be closely bound by data and figures. But reality dictates otherwise. Philadelphia's problem, no less than the nation's, is to come off a low in spirit and self-confidence that will pervade the Bicentennial Year.

It is also quite beyond the writer's mind frame to envision some comprehensive view of a day so far distant. Even the Club of Rome's computer stops fifty years ahead. Rather than a detailed model, my own approach instead will build on four assumptions and will deal more with concepts than concrete pictures of the future.

The first assumption is that tomorrow will be shaped by what we do today. We board a moving train of history, which has been handsomely portrayed in the earlier chapters. It is wise to look around its cars for clues to future prospects and events. Steps taken in the early years ahead will sharply affect later outcomes. For this reason, sections of this chapter pick up themes derived from past and present and examine their application to the future.

A second assumption is that what happens in Philadelphia a hundred years from now will be determined in only limited degree by events that occur within the city or that are made by Philadelphians. The city is already caught well within a web of national and international events. While there will continue to be localized political decisions and a range of distinctly Philadelphia institutions, and while land use and civic design will still have a local flavor, Philadelphia's broad economic base and its overall quality of life—including the attitudes and outlooks of its people—will be more influenced by events of worldwide magnitude: by decisions reached, ideas hatched and technologies devised in places around the world, and by natural and man-made catastrophes that have always confounded the course of history. Much of this chapter will therefore deal with national rather than uniquely local responses likely at some future time.

A third assumption supplies a measure of hope. It is a deep respect for the place of cycles in the tides of history and the life of great cities. The layman can spot relentless variations on the same themes through time. Recessions, reforms, fashions and neighborhood popularity are all subject to ups and downs. Issues and ideas commanding public attention emerge and slide away, to return some years later. As individuals living and reacting at a point in time, we are caught in these tides and often forget that times change.

The cycles of history are irrefutable reminders of the constancy of the underlying human condition. This recognition illumines as well the unique contribution of individuals and the repeated emergence through time of fresh ideas and attitudes that can transform troughs of despair into peaks of achievement. There can be a rapid emergence of new forces capable of changing the downward slope of any curves we might draw on Philadelphia's present graph of life quality. As Rene Dubos, the noted microbiologist, has said, "Trend is not destiny." To have effect upon the contemporary scene, these new forces must reach beyond technology or momentary political victories and generate a new set of individual goals and attitudes. There must develop a new metaphysical basis through which future Philadelphians may explain and relate themselves to the human condition that they now experience.

The fourth assumption follows. The demands of the underlying human condition must be central to our future plans. Neither land use, nor dollars, nor "programs," nor technology, nor design, nor other organizing principles we have utilized in the past can supply the necessary regenerative force. Philadelphia, through 200 years, has become very different in skyline, life tempo, economic base and status in the family of cities. But it is very much the same when viewed in human terms. The basic requirements of all Philadelphians for self-esteem and recognition, for love, for variety and choice, for periods of rest and activity, for both freedom and security exist as they did 200 years ago and still dominate individual and collective responses.

The bureaucrats of 2076 will behave much as ours do now. So will the professionals, the retailers, the unemployed and other groupings of Philadelphians. Whether our polity becomes more level or pyramidal, man's self-interest, his sense of the tragic and the absurd and his need to know the "why" of his existence will remain unchanged. The use of technology and science will have, then as now, an upper limit in satisfying the underlying needs and problems of mankind.

THE AMERICAN DEMOCRATIC FAITH: THEN AND NOW

The Founding Fathers shared similar assumptions, although in far simpler times. They were versed in the requirements and frailties of colonial Americans, their would-be countrymen. This is evidenced in the documents they wrote in Philadelphia. It permeates the goals set for the noble experiment in democracy. Broad boundaries were placed upon the new nation's governing institutions but great leeway was allowed for their detailed application through changing times. The allowance for evolution is the genius of the system created in Philadelphia. The more we examine these products the more we note their relevance to life in Philadelphia today.

Whether tested at the time of the writing of the Declaration of Independence or at intervals since 1776, a basic theme of the American way of life has always been that human affairs should be thought of in terms of the individual.

Historians have described the simple patterns of individualism in early American life, whether on the frontier or in rapidly growing cities like Philadelphia. In each setting, the home was the centerpoint of life and the individual's lot was sacred. There was room to move upward and outward. Self-interest was relentlessly pursued. Public instruments were kept to a minimum. Jefferson and later Emerson placed their confidence in continuing education and the civility of the individual, whose progress under a fundamental moral law would check the need for greater public authority. The validity of the ethic of American individualism was daily confirmed in an uncrowded, secure and lush environment. Progress appeared inevitable.

Under such conditions—both physical and psychological—the nation boomed. By 1800 Philadelphia was still the second-largest city in the English-speaking world. By 1850 rail lines stretched westward from Philadelphia and the wealth of the hinterlands made the city a center of prosperity.

America was a colossal incubator. The frontier, Frederick Jackson Turner would argue, was the determining force in American life, with tremendous impact both upon the building of cities and the attitudes, expectations and behavior of Americans. Philadelphia was caught in the evolution and became a magnet for tens of thousands of newcomers. For the waves of immigrants who flocked to Philadelphia, individual opportunity amid unknown freedom was the lure.

In global terms, Philadelphia became one of the world's newest, richest suburbs. Despite adverse living conditions and a sometimes spiteful attitude toward newer arrivals, the immigrants stayed on and the city grew and prospered. Bitter but passing confrontations developed over access to land, housing and amenities, but the success of the vast majority reinforced the faith. The message was incontestable. The free individual could make it in Philadelphia, could come to assume political and economic power and could find pride and self-esteem in his or her city of adoption.

By 1976, however, the waves of immigration have almost ceased. This facet of the frontier has virtually ended. Laws now limit the influx from abroad. The word is out that worthwhile opportunities in cities like Philadelphia are scarce. The northward migration of native blacks has ceased. Only small trickles of hispanic Americans and orientals reverse the flow. The spring of immigration and urban migration is drying up in terms the decennial census can calculate.

But the psychological pull of the frontier on Philadelphia remains strong. Large numbers of Philadelphians continue to move to the suburbs or beyond, or leave for other parts of the country where opportunity looms larger. The drive of the free individual to move upward and outward persists as if stamped upon the American's genetic code.

The effects of the frontier mentality will be a major determinant of Philadelphia's future in the twenty-first century. It now propels a massive centrifugal force, moving the city's residents to the edge of their city or beyond. For forty years it has been viewed in largely racial terms, but is better regarded as part of the free individual's persistent search for income, status and opportunity. It is a glacial force propelled by public policy, by powerful advertisement and the absence of strong incentives to remain behind except for the very wealthy.

Thus Germantown, Hunting Park and Wynnefield today feel the pressure of families to move up and to square the reality of their lives with the models they see on television, read about in magazines and drive by in their cars. Tomorrow the Northeast, Merion and Swarthmore will feel similar pressures which, by then, will be moderated by simultaneous events of profound magnitude. The coercion of the energy crisis will be a counter-force to outward movement. Its rate will be adjusted by the persistence of a declining birth rate, the absence of a fresh wave of newcomers in the inner city and a continuing leveling of incomes. A gradual melting of the racial aspect of the glacier will take place. It would be accelerated by a direct effort to de-market the allure of the frontier and to sell the advantages of city living for the free individual in the twenty-first century.

A central planning question for the future is what will become of Philadelphia's inner land areas beyond the central business district once its beachhead role for newcomers has concluded. The answer will turn upon the impact of new concepts of life style, convenience and amenity, born of fresh attitudes about the world and fueled by the growing shortage of low-cost fuel. The holes in the present land use donut will hopefully be filled in time by free individuals seeking new options, based on the variety and choice that cities have always provided in history. Examples are already appearing in diverse neighborhoods like Powelton Village, Society Hill, Fairmount and South Street. These are new incubators arising out of a postfrontier consideration of life values and strong enough to fly in the face of the stereotypes of adverse urban conditions.

Rationality was a second strand woven deeply into the American democratic faith from day one of the Republic. The framers of the nation were, for good reason, confident in themselves and in the power of human reason and initiative. They were rationalists with intellectual roots in the Enlightenment. Their frame of attention was the individual man. Reason, rather than mysticism or Freudian psychology, was central to their thinking. The central notion of democracy—government by the consent of the governed—squared with their lot and their distance from sources of authority. It was strongly influenced by John Locke's concept of a benign relationship between man and nature, whose validity was plausibly confirmed in the rich, fresh and secure environment of their new land.

During the first century of independence, rationality verged on becoming a state religion. Faith in the nation's legitimacy and the efficacy of its institutions was broadly based. The primacy of law, the system of checks and balances and the notion of limited sovereignty were working, despite occasional fits and starts. Abstract principles of moral law and order were felt to undergird all society. The children of the republic were taught that the moral order in turn derived from God, and not merely from man. For nonbelievers, there was an abstract acceptance of similar laws derived from nature. Locke's theories, the Bill of Rights and God's providence over America became as one and inseparable as the union. While graft, smoke-filled rooms and bitter election campaigns were being fought out at one level, a near religious faith in American governmental institutions and in rational decision-making prevailed at another.

Constant reinforcement of this faith was being personally experienced by most Americans, in the same way that the richness of his land reinforces the faith of the Lancaster County farmer. Besides Philadelphians, like all Americans, were blissfully isolated in their hemispheric incubator. All news about life quality elsewhere in the world confirmed the faith. So did the series of revolutionary steps in Europe to emulate the American experience. Such evidence helped to unify an increasingly diversified population.

Today that element of faith in the workings of just and rational institutions has fallen from the heavens. Much empirical evidence presents an easy reascendance. Laws, once clearly above the rulers of the moment, seem less so now, despite the gratifying results of the Watergate experience. Faith in eternal right and wrong has been replaced by pragmatism, expediency, cost-benefit analysis and the balancing of power. The protective coating on the American democratic faith has been removed.

It is now fashionable to think in "value-free" terms about matters of public policy and future planning. A scientific gospel created the present economic base of the country. Analysis, objectivity and improving techniques of quantification have become major tools of our society. Scientific management, so much the basis of our industrial know-how, was first applied in Philadelphia's Midvale Steel Company. More recently, "planning-programming-budgeting-systems," electronic data processing and greater productivity are ideas that have been transferred from private to public institutions in the best traditions of bringing rational method to government. But the use of such tools is occurring even as the goals they would measure and optimize become more difficult to agree upon. The synthesizing, almost unquestioned force of the prior faith currently eludes us.

There is little present agreement on the values to be stressed in laying plans for Philadelphia's neighborhoods or transportation system, for the scope of instruction to be offered in its schools or in the basic allocation of public dollars. The everyday experience of many Philadelphians suggests real limits upon the attainment of economic opportunity, higher incomes and space. Even in the 1960's, the determined optimism of "The New Frontier," (and later the Great Society) failed in large measure because they did not seem to square with a sense by many Philadelphians that the leeway and expectations of "The Old Frontier" no longer applied in their mature, static city. The programs were rationally conceived to aid the impoverished individual and to assist his upward mobility. The programs were a disappointment, not simply for lack of good management or insufficient funding as some have argued, but because they did not reach deeper feelings of alienation, outrage and a growing sense of superfluousness on the part of many Americans. The programs of a new rationality thus sometimes bred irrational responses and frustrations.

In Philadelphia, a grass roots recognition of the changing nature of the real frontier in America has preceded government's or the establishment's responses. It has made the celebration of the Bicentennial difficult for many citizens. Supporters seem to be turning back the clock or hiding in symbols that no longer command automatic allegiance because they no longer square with today's reality. The average Philadelphian knows that nostalgia will not suffice to build the future while, at the same time, he or she yearns for renewed evidence that the system works and that he or she is a part of it.

In the next century, Philadelphians will have escaped from the outworn frontier mentality and, in so doing, will be building a new faith that rests on values and symbols appropriate for life in the twenty-first century. The centrality of the free individuality and faith in rationality will persist, but they will be modified concepts that face the fact that Philadelphia has become a mature city in a mature nation, both within a world with discernible, if distant limits.

The noble experiment of 1776 and its later success engendered a national sense of mission. America exported not only its goods and services but also its democratic principles. The impact on world institutions has been truly remarkable. This sense of mission developed religious overtones, sometimes amalgamated with a drive to protect economic interests and sometimes for territorial gain. This concept of manifest destiny is found symbolized in Philadelphia: in many statues, in the presence of Admiral Dewey's flagship that entered Manila harbor, in the navy yard itself.

The proud mission of America was never stronger than in the two world wars and their aftermath. The Marshall Plan was perhaps its most noble and effective expression; the Peace Corps, a smaller, later model.

The Vietnam War, which brought about the deaths of many young Philadelphians, saw the overreaching of this sense of mission. Again, individuals felt it more quickly than did governmental leaders. The consequence was a crushing realization for many Philadelphians and their countrymen that our life style and institutions are not exportable to many newly developing nations, whose faith must square with different meanings of reality.

Sitting at the top of the heap of nations, moreover, is found to be a vulnerable and uncomfortable position. Other patriots now apply the very words to our President that the Founding Fathers used to describe the colonists' tormentors. A cycle of history is closing. In self-interest, America remains the protector of the free world but our missionary zeal has sharply waned.

Long before 2076, all Philadelphians will understand these changes. We will have learned to see this city as a world city, one of 300 or more with a population above a million people. We will have learned it through incessant struggles to allocate scarce natural resources and, in all probability, through more than one world tragedy or war.

In the years before 2076, the economic base of Philadelphia will depend increasingly on world markets and the political attitudes of emerging nations. The fate of the dollar will be increasingly limited to political decisions made in Tokyo and Cairo, Peking and Sao Paulo. A world reserve bank will have emerged among the trading nations. Our petroleum supply will have long since vanished, having been used and abused for momentary gain. No longer able to buy what we desire—products, commodities, art and talent—we already feel the emergence of a new world of limits and competition. The United States is already passing from a short period as the world's dominant power, even as Philadelphia soon passed as the nation's premier city.

There is physical evidence of these changes at hand. Philadelphia's role as a rail hub diminishes in importance, even as its port and airport facilities steadily grow. The latter will continue to prosper in the years ahead. Room for expansion will become available as huge land areas occupied by refineries and the navy yard become expendable. The ports of the Delaware River, Ameriport, will rival Europort in activity in the years ahead. Philadelphia's pivotal location at the center of the Eastern corridor will be like Rotterdam's in Western Europe.

Further speculation suggests that many local corporations and other institutions will have passed to international control, in the same way that this century has seen the demise of locally owned firms and their replacement by multinational leadership. Such infusions of new talent and perspectives will, on balance, be favorable to the city.

Concurrently, such shifts will set up the opposing force of still greater population mobility and alliances among the cities of the world. The acceleration of technological homogenization will surely increase on a world scale. Not only will churches be a somewhat universal common denominator in the cities of the world, but so will hotels, housing units, television programming and schooling.

It follows that Philadelphia will be dotted with the offices of many international institutions. The faces on its sidewalks will be more cosmopolitan than now. Thousands of students from around the world will be drawn here. Transient populations will increase in the wake of travel and commercial relationships. This movement will be a two-way street. Native Philadelphians will think little or nothing of moving to Dar es Salaam or Sydney, as they do now to Chicago. Local schools will expand their teaching of foreign languages and cultures. English will no longer have sole supremacy in the world of nations. National survival may require a mastery of Chinese, Russian, Arabic and Portuguese as well.

As world interchange increases, we will see the companion growth of a movement to preserve and enhance local history and traditions. Here Philadelphia can profit more than most American cities. Its present efforts to preserve its historic past give it a headstart as an antidote to mindless homogenization and as a lure to visitors. Mummery, our black history, soft pretzels and Georgian architecture will become more precious to all Philadelphians. Conservation will be a new expression of distinctiveness and individuality, as well as vital to the economic base of the future.

In short, by 2076 Philadelphians will have permanently adjusted to a new role in an interdependent globe. The United States will have become a trading partner and not principally an exporter of ideas and institutional forms. Its democratic concepts will remain valid but there will be a greater willingness to import ideas from other nations of the world, both large and small. Philadelphia will accept and adapt to many of these imported changes.

A final feature of the nation's independence period has entirely vanished in 1976 and will never return to color the American democratic faith of the future. For the better part of two centuries, a sense of national security was a distinctly American possession. Except at its own hand and among its own citizens, the United States has escaped the ravages of war on its own soil. While Philadelphia has its quota of granite monuments commemorating its war dead from seven conflicts, no quarter of the city has been destroyed by enemy bombs. The last battle fought in Philadelphia was the Battle of Germantown, in revolution against the British. If portions of the city look bombed out, it is through our own abandonment and proligate use of resources, a product of the frontier mind.

Today enemy missiles are trained on Philadelphia. Once protected from possible adversaries by mighty oceans, our security is now the product of delicate and shifting power relationships and the nation's wealth, which has given to it a strong defense through technology. Looking ahead, it is highly conceivable that one or more American cities will be destroyed within the century, through a decision made by rivals in the struggle for the world's resources or by tragic miscalculation.

An hourly threat thus hangs over the city in 1976. The threat generates a psychological strain that saps our spirit as well as our budgets. There is also the cruel irony that Americans to date have been the sole users of nuclear weaponry. We can argue the deterrent results of that demonstration in World War II, but the fact remains that a critical element of national pride was simultaneously exploded.

There is in 1976 literally no place left to hide or run. Long before 2076, all Americans will know that to be true. Philadelphians' attitudes and behavior will reflect the new condition.

To summarize, the American democratic faith, which was framed in Philadelphia, has for 200 years been continually tested as an organizing principle for personal, community or national use. The need for a faith—a binding force of goals and values responsive to the individual's concept of reality—remains unaltered. It is reality in Philadelphia and elsewhere that has changed, and so must the substance of the faith itself. America is no longer an isolated incubator or a land of perpetual progress. The individual is even more free to pursue his private self-interest but his expectations contain a growing sense of outward boundaries. The frontier, both physical and psychological, is passing or has passed.

The requirement for the next hundred years is to redefine a faith that is consistent with postfrontier conditions. This adaptation will be the major theme unfolding in Philadelphia in the years ahead. The balance of this chapter will try to indicate how key points in the earlier American democratic faith might become consistent with tomorrow's realities.

PHILADELPHIA ON THE POSTFRONTIER

In probing the future, physical aspects are the easiest to envision. They come naturally to every child who has played with blocks and designed his or her own cities. They contain the frequently confirmed assumption that physical change can induce far-reaching changes in our culture.

In the 1950's and 1960's, Edmund Bacon skillfully used the power of design concepts to mobilize fresh attitudes toward physical change and the future of Philadelphia. The concepts were made real by other gifted planners and architects. The psychological impact of these plans was vast, particularly as pieces like Penn Center and Penn's Landing have taken shape. Dozens of American cities have since built their own Penn Centers. These projects graphically expressed common goals, despite strong differences among the city's citizens. They produced pride and sources of identification. The design ideas were not themselves sustained by deep analysis and data quantification. They were intuitive, holistic. They were used by enlightened political leadership as part of the fuel of reform.

Remnants of the power of these concepts persist today, a quarter-century later. It is strong testament to their clarity and to the collective need for symbols that they filled. Some projects like Market East are yet unfolding, although the *raison d'être* has changed in the intervening years. For the most part, however, physical symbols of direction and common purpose no longer enjoy the public's confidence in the face of persistent poverty, pathology and political change. Our attention has shifted to more fundamental aspects of city life and to a new search for common values.

One physical symbol that does survive, interestingly, is the statue of William Penn atop City Hall. In Philadelphia, it remains unwritten law that no structure shall exceed the height of Penn's hat. The rule serves as a respected symbol of self-restraint and balance, which has done much to temper the scale of living in Philadelphia. The statue says that Philadelphia's physical shape shall be dictated by the measure of a man!

The measure of man will be the essential measure of the postfrontier period. Beyond application to physical scale, it will become the denominator of all activities that comprise the city's life. This must reach the metaphysical or attitudinal level as well.

It has been said already that the essential parameters of the human condition will remain unchanged a hundred years from now. It is the physical and economic setting of man that will be drastically different, largely because of man's own actions. Philadelphians, long distinguished in medical and behavioral studies, will continue to probe the edges of life's mystery but the key dimensions of the human animal will remain essentially unchanged. Residents of 2006 or 2076 will still be primarily affected by their strong instincts to survive, to find self-respect, to love and have attachments to others, and to minimize the inconvenience and danger quotients in their lives. In 2076 there will still be shallow persons, craven persons, venal and jealous persons. The classic typologies of mankind will live on, whether described in humors, the latest psychiatric lingo or technological measurements. As in Penn's, Franklin's and Dilworth's Philadelphia, residents will seek to find an equilibrium in their physical, mental and spiritual requirements.

But they will do so under more exacting and restrictive conditions and demands. By dint of living well within an interdependent world with established boundaries to its essential systems, the average Philadelphian will require a deeper sense of selfhood and individuality than is required even today. How well he or she copes with this requirement will be the critical determinant of the city's future character and its survival. For many, it will be a profoundly difficult adjustment. New levels of discipline, tolerance and mutual respect will be required. There is concurrent opportunity for this adaptation to produce both a new and binding set of societal goals and personal grounds for faith in themselves and their institutions.

There have always been numbers of Philadelphians who were not making it in the sense of participating in the life and satisfactions of their contemporaries. There have always been the poor, the handicapped, the retarded and others unable to live at the prevalent tempo of city living. In simpler times, we saw less of them. They were cared for in private homes, by relatives, friends and neighbors. As population and the pace of life accelerated, Philadelphians responded compassionately to their less self-sufficient fellow citizens. Through churches and charities, through self-help and ethnic groups, assistance was forthcoming. Penn himself set a noble standard by his tolerance of the disadvantaged and nonconforming of his day. Franklin left personal funds to give food and fuel to the poor. The record of the Quakers, centered in Philadelphia, is a world legend in humanitarianism. The role of Philadelphians in the abolition movement was outstanding.

In recent years, giving here as elsewhere has become a public function or centralized in united ways of voluntary assistance. Human resource programs have become the fastest-growing parts of the city budget. A security blanket of health and welfare benefits has been woven, both by government and by private sector institutions.

At the physical and material levels, there is no question that those in need are better cared for, despite enormous gaps that remain in public and private programs. The same improvement may not, however, hold in terms of personal evaluation and a full sense of membership in the larger community. While we have extended life for many, we have also, however unwittingly, seen the value of individual life become cheapened for many more.

The extended family has virtually disappeared. Instead, the elderly are placed in nursing homes, to live out their days in custodial care. Thousands of parents look to schools for far more than the teaching of basic skills, only to find that neither reading levels nor equipment with which to face life's choices are received by their children.

The nuclear family suffers as well in the stress of modern urban conditions. The black family's problems have been accorded special attention, but strain on all family structure receives more and more notice. Public programs have all too frequently produced extreme levels of individual dependency upon government and faceless institutions. Violence, a feature of the first frontier, has become part of our way of life. Resulting fears reduce the city's collective willingness and capacity to cope.

Despite quantifiable improvements along a hundred measurable indicators of life quality, postfrontier Philadelphia faces the basic question of how to eliminate a feeling among growing numbers that life itself has little apparent purpose, mystery or demand upon them as individuals. A central question for many current residents of the city is why they should even get up in the morning.

Another way to state this is to say that 10 to 15 percent of Philadelphia's citizens are today superfluous to our city's way of life. This percentage includes most often—but not exclusively—its poor, newest arrived, unskilled and others wounded by contacts with the city's institutions. Their ranks also include the very sensitive, for whom present institutions have no appeal, attachment or reward. There is evidence that many workers in production lines and clerical pools begin to place themselves in this same category.

Many of these individuals are superfluous in the strictest economic sense as well. We have learned to "cost out" this population and to determine that their measurable assets do not meet the costs of supporting them. This was not the case in labor-short colonial America where all had jobs or did not survive, nor is it so in Western Europe today where labor is in short supply and even the brain-damaged have a role in the economy.

The effect of these equations is viewed in budget cuts and constant efforts to reduce the costs of many accepted programs. The impact of these actions reinforces in many individuals their sense of superfluousness. Thus the gang youth, the welfare mother, the drug addict and countless others feel estranged from the city, its systems and its symbols. They write it in grafitti and act it out in violence or withdrawal.

Unless we move to a more inclusive system, we risk adding thousands more to the ranks of the self-convinced superfluous in the years ahead and further contributing to a cheapening of life. Such a trend negates the nation's central faith in the role of the free individual. Moreover, the latent resources and energy of those presumed surplus stand in stark contrast to the growing awareness of material and natural shortages, as well as to the inadequate quality of living in our city. The presumed superfluous represent an enormous pool with whom to achieve socially useful aims.

The future requires conversion of their numbers into social assets or major disruptions in the life of Philadelphia will result. There must be continuing evidence of political, social and economic efforts to accept them and their drives to attain personal equilibrium under urban conditions. This process of urban alchemy must take place while respecting the range of abilities and desires among the city's total population and while operating amid a steady barrage of information and experience that daily tests the individual's conclusions about how he or she is faring.

When Jefferson was secretary of state, he required intelligence from his ambassador to Spain as the world situation threatened to deteriorate and draw the young nation into unwelcome war with France and England. Jefferson dispatched a courier by boat to Spain to obtain the needed advice. Months later, the courier returned and the necessary decisions were made. The peace was preserved.

Today's world brooks no such leisurely intervals in making personal or public decisions or evaluations. Minutes, not days or weeks, become critical in the life of individuals, cities and nations. Philadelphians daily feel the commanding roles played in their lives by the print and electronic media. Journalists and advertising men are the arbiters of taste and fashion. They make and break leadership. They see and hear and reduce the world to digestible segments for us.

Philadelphians several generations hence will be better adapted to the barrage of information and the coercion of data than are its residents today. Children are already far better adapted to television than are their parents. They are able to sort out its messages. The greatest single role for new technology will be in supplementing our limited mental equipment to understand the vast and complex issues of our times and how we relate to them. The computer, first invented in Philadelphia, will be the principal tool in this development.

The Philadelphia preacher, Russell Conwell, in his famous speech, "Acres of Diamonds," celebrated the doctrine of the free individual. "Money is power," said Conwell in 1888, and went on to argue that securing wealth was an honorable goal through which to do good in the world. He became an apologist for the rugged individualism of nineteenth century America, translating the doctrine of the free individual into the material, industrial period in which Philadelphia played a leading role. Money was then the key to power and success.

Before 2076, control of information will have replaced money as the principal vehicle of power and influence in postfrontier America. The individual's range of disposable income will have been markedly limited at either end of the spectrum, even as artificial differences of ethnic origin and sex are minimized among Philadelphia's residents. Information and how it is used to affect a person's equilibrium and the spirit of the city will become the principal ingredients affecting security and societal adaptation. It its handling will lie the very definition of reality itself and a source of immense power.

THE PROSPECTS FOR ADAPTATION

There are ample reasons to suggest that our attainment of a basic equilibrium as a city can indeed occur despite impressive evidence to the contrary. The best evidence is supplied by the record of the past. Whatever its unevenness and the costs of its attainment, lines of clearly improving life quality and inclusiveness can be drawn between the earlier chapters in this volume. They show rising indices of personal income, health, education and access to both opportunity and information. This has occurred despite cycles of setback and confrontation.

It is only at the level of personal faith, inner security and a sense of quality that we must draw a steadily sinking line. But even in this regard today's conditions may be favorable to build new attitudes that are consistent with our classic faith as Americans. And to argue that such developments might be led by Philadelphia is not preposterous. It happened once, in 1776, and through the years the city has had an uncanny knack of playing host to seminal ideas affecting American thought and action.

A first ingredient of a new and operable faith will stem from a revised definition of the concept of rationality itself. It will be a product of the very increase in our access to information. Instead of a clock-like world based upon primitive scientific specualtion about the basic laws of nature, the evolving statement will be based on a well-recognized regard for the interlocking nature of the world's systems. Confirmed by computer, trips to the moon and now by the politics of scarce resource allocation, a new rationality is emerging from a closer, first-hand knowledge of our limitations and their impact on human behavior. Proponents of holistic thinking are today's descendants of John Locke. This is the symbolism of Spaceship Earth. Philadelphians begin to see for themselves the links between food, population, petroleum and air. We already begin to realize the interdependence between Philadelphia and the rest of the world, between man and nature.

Constant corroboration that these systems exist and that nature's balance is essentially fragile will give Philadelphians a richer sense of the individual's position in life than had their deist forefathers. Philadelphians like Ian McHarg and Ruth Patrick today articulate the complex balance of these systems and give us greater respect for the workings of this modern clock. Our eco-system's future capacity to permit global and personal equilibrium depends upon grasping these concepts and in using our power to balance man and nature; above all, to respect the limits of the world by which we are bounded.

A hundred years ago, a Philadelphian named Henry George declared war on conditions that he felt made man superfluous in his day. George's concept of a single tax stemmed from the basic conclusion, expressed in terms of the American democratic faith then operative, that God gave man the right to use the earth and the lands thereof for all people's benefit. George thus proposed the public appropriation of the unearned increment in value which is created on the land. Through it, the state would become the equalizer of rich and poor. George lived his entire life promoting this accounting system and method of reform to benefit man in proper measure.

Philadelphia will need a new accounting system to face the twenty-first century. In sharp contrast to the detail with which we calculate the costs of goods and services and other facets of our economic life, we do not yet place comparable values upon many vital components of life quality. Air, light, the ocean waters and inspiring views have no readily measurable translation into our calculation of cost and benefit, even though their quantity is finite.

But these are not the central factors now omitted. Man himself, the essence of our democratic faith, is born with no "dollar value" and thus there is no way to measure his place within our total system of accounts. How many decisions we make would be quite different if each individual carried a certain dollar value . . . call it his life capital? In holistic terms, our accounting systems are truncated until we can include the individual in computing the total assets of our finite world and before making trade-offs in our use of all resources, personal and material.

Today fringe benefits, working conditions and "psychic income" are parts of an expanding accounting system through which we attempt to measure the overall quality of life. Insurance companies translate this concept furthest into figures affecting the individual. More capricious efforts are found in the bargaining involved in negligence and malpractice cases, in which the value of an individual's life is often computed. As we face reality about what endures and is reusable, as opposed to what is ephemeral, our accounting system will further shift.

Long before 2076 we will have developed a far better system of total accounting. It will permit us to judge the long-term consequences of short-term decisions and thus protect many of our resources from premature exhaustion. As we have come to value land and have assessed different kinds of construction, so will we have learned to assess many new values now taken for granted. There will be a new balance sheet in which both man's costs and his values will be measured. With such tools, we will be able to establish the status of an ever-shifting equilibrium in our society and our city.

Once we understand the rational working of the "world clock" of which we are a component part, components of the classic American democratic faith, other than rationality, also take on new meaning.

In contemporary Philadelphia, the need for a new social contract, incorporating both conventional and currently intangible factors, has been most clearly felt among the city's growing black population, whose life conditions have forced a constant confrontation with today's reality. The term "superfluous people" has been applied to black Americans in recent years. Now, insistence by black leadership that there be a new concept of humanity and self-identification, as well as the material resources with which to share more equitably in the total society, advances the general effort to adapt to changing times and to find new symbols. The slogans and goals of the civil rights movement are like the ones that emerged in colonial America.

In the 1950's and 1960's, Philadelphia's black population became the chief evaluators of the city's quality of living: its housing, its educational services and the structures in its economic system. Martin Luther King's dream was the American democratic faith restated at the closing of the old frontier period. The nation's failure, no less a failure in this city, produced a peaceful revolution that continues. Selective patronage was thus devised in Philadelphia to force an end to job discrimination. The Opportunities Industrialization Center was founded here by Leon Sullivan to train black workers to overcome the handicaps of their environment so they could accept jobs opened to them.

The initial response, both locally and nationally, was to allocate new resources for compensatory education, housing and other programs. New dollars from governments at all levels were willingly applied, and in no place more energetically than in Philadelphia. The operations of city government were changed and new agencies and regulatory activities were set in motion. The public schools moved rapidly to shift the center of attention to the black majority of their pupils.

In the ensuing adjustments caused by these efforts, it soon became clear that these moves encroached upon places occupied by other citizens. A series of confrontations arose that still persist. Fresh evidence of limits upon the role of the free individual in urban America was revealed.

For a brief period, a false frontier of vastly higher expectations held the favor of public opinion. While some might argue that the ratio between goals and results was disappointing because sufficient resources were not applied, others argue that the needed total resources were simply not there and that, in pursuit of the American democratic faith, good intentions were allowed to shield actual possibilities from view. In 1976, we are beginning to acknowledge that fact and its corollary: that our combined resources as a city—public and private, personal and material—must be stretched and better managed and assigned.

In 1976 we also find other groups of individuals working to attain or to retain goals comparable to those espoused by minority groups and to make a restatement of their own individuality. Polish, Italian, female and gay Philadelphians have joined in conscious efforts to work out their place in the dawning world beyond the false frontier of unlimited expectations. In this defensive and protective period, so characterized by the present city administration, deep-seated human forces have gathered strength and will not be denied. Fresh waves of change begin to build even as we begin to see the reality of the adjustments that can be accomplished over time.

Added evidence of individual desires to preserve freedom and to restore a sense of balance is found in other contemporary movements. What has become the environmental movement was triggered by a growing awareness of the misuse of natural resources, of ruined quality amid plenty. Birth of the movement was celebrated in Philadelphia during Earth Week, 1970, when 100,000 Philadelphians flocked to Fairmount Park in a spontaneous demonstration of the delicate link perceived between man and his environment.

In the past six years, the environmental movement has managed to put a stop to highway and other public projects felt to be contrary to newly emerging values. Government agencies have again proliferated. The environmental impact statement has emerged as a regulatory tool. At the same time, a new respect for hands-on work, for natural foods, for endangered species and for the self-sufficiency of the family farm have developed.

As yet these are tentative and partial responses, not held by the bulk of Philadelphians or other Americans. It is far too early to say that a new synthesis has emerged, as adjustment to the energy crisis clearly demonstrates. Tough choices proliferate, testing the old frontier against the dawning reality of scarcity. Should Philadelphia tap the outer continental shelf to fuel its cars and industries, or should it hold fast, given possible environmental hazards? During the ensuing one hundred years, we will have better learned how to operate our spaceship and to calculate its course between such choices, or have failed in our adaptation process.

The consumer movement supplies additional evidence of the strength of the free individual in search of equilibrium. A lack of access and relief in dealings with both public and private institutions is broadly experienced. Philadelphians are demanding quality and honest dealings in the marketplace and with regard to standards of product quality and consumer safety. Epitomized by Ralph Nader, the consumer movement rests well within the American democratic faith and its material emphasis. It is less concerned with fewer cars than safer cars; it is more concerned with honest advertising than with the need for many of the products themselves. Quality control is its theme in seeking to protect the citizen and the consumer against the excesses of firms and fellow citizens who profit from the increasing facelessness of the marketplace. The consumer movement is part of our adaptation process and will grow steadily in the years ahead until governmental reform and a new sense of corporate responsibility take place on a large scale.

A fourth strand to be worked out in the years ahead concerns the question of limits to the numbers of individuals themselves. Advocates of population control, whether by restraint, contraception or abortion, face up quite directly to the concept of limits in our world society. Sharp drops in the birth rate suggest that the urgency of this adjustment has been accepted by most Americans despite continuing acrimony over acceptable means of control. Despite this evidence, conflicting positions are held in the name of "the free individual" and "the quality of life," which are simultaneously argued to be the salvation and the destruction of man.

By 2076 Philadelphia will have learned to live within an atmosphere of limits. The integrity of the world's majestic and delicate systems will be respected, or we will have perished. Our success in doing so will be determined by the picture of reality we carry in our heads. Philadelphians will have had to substitute fresh images for ones that no longer hold true. Progress will continue to be made but not without a constant exchange of costs and benefits. The stereotype of perpetual and imminent progress and unlimited resources will first need to be replaced.

The concept of the bell-shaped curve provides a useful image to synthesize the impact of the foregoing considerations, both as they relate to our democratic faith and to future living quality considerations in Philadelphia. By 2076, it is vital that the image of the bell-shaped curve be as fully accepted as a symbol of our societal goals as the Liberty Bell has become a symbol of the origins of our faith.

In statistical terms, the bell-shaped curve reflects the normal distribution of a given universe of elements or qualities. Thus a jar of fruit flies will, when counted, display a bell-shaped range of wing size, eye coloration and the like. Or a universe of blood donors will show a bell-shaped curve.

A bell-shaped curve can also be drawn to describe the distribution of Philadelphians as they seek to achieve life, liberty and the pursuit of happiness. Today, approximately two million dots together form the city's curve for any key indicator of life quality such as income, educational attainment or occupation. The ideal, although not actual, distribution would show a large group of these dots clustered in the middle ranges and smaller numbers tapering off at either end. The position occupied under the curve by any individual will be the product of his personal capabilities (among them, aptitude, motivation and experience) interacting with a variety of constantly-shifting political, social and economic forces and relationships.

On any given day, a snapshot of the actual distribution of Philadelphians will show a distortion of the ideal or bell-shaped distribution. Yet, according to the American democratic faith, any individual is free to move within the overall limits of the curve without artifical restriction or man-made discrimination. No one is to be penalized from moving just as far as his capabilities will take him or her.

The bell-shaped curve symbolizes both limits governing the overall range of individual possibilities, while demonstrating ample room for personal movement, fair access, and an opportunity to achieve excellence. It is thus a symbol for living in a post-frontier society and for facing up to the total interaction of our finite resources, man-made and natural.

Measured by past performance, one's location under this curve a hundred years from now will more closely correspond to individual capability. Artificial and discredited determinants of sex, ethnicity and race will have been displaced. Income will be of lesser consequence. Men and women will maneuver for position far more equally. The legal system, the adaptive tools provided by the Bill of Rights, will be used to see that the sorting process takes place with maximum fairness and with equity.

The crucial difference, then and now, will be more certain knowledge by every Philadelphian that there are boundaries on his or her life and a correspondingly greater respect for the essential, often difficult transactions that must take place between individuals. Government's increasing role will be to assure a more ideal, hence normal, distribution to take place. Some called "poor" will still be with us but only in a relative sense and with far less disconnection from the mainstream of the income curve of all citizens. Taxation and other modes of public policy will have further limited the extremes of the income picture through redistributive mechanisms, some already in the plans of legislative committees and advocate groups. These adjustments, however, will take effect only after strong resistance from those who are displaced in some relative sense from their present position under the bell-shaped curve.

Essential to living in a world of more readily conceived limits will be allowance for conditions under which individuals may work out acceptable ways to endure, at worst, and to enjoy, wherever possible, the changing complexity of their world. In Roman times, the catacomb was the breeding ground for the Christian community. Puritans and other nonconformists found similar oases in the cities of England and the Continent. The New World was itself an escape to fresh horizons in which new life-giving spirit could emerge. America was not only a land for the free and the brave but also for the nonconformist and the restless.

These times represent a similar watershed in human events, except there is no fresh new world to receive a similar, restless population. A renewal and reformulating process must continue, however, if human kind is to adapt and to survive. New societal tissue must be continually built. While black separateness, the communes and the swarming together of other like individuals in Philadelphia seem strange or even worrisome to those already at the centerpoint of the bell-shaped curve, they should be viewed as points en route to a new synthesis and distribution. They are means through which numbers of individuals are reexamining their connections with reality. The drug addict, in the healing environment of a therapeutic community, sees his experience as a way to redefine his life and to live again.

Philadelphia is constantly reviving in this manner. Once abolition societies, turnvereins, mummers' clubs and gentlemen's eating societies performed this role. More recently, labor unions, civil rights groups and block clubs have flourished. For some, the place they work has become the central point of association and the nature of the place of work is changing as a result. Other stabs at finding new points of personal equilibrium include singles bars, new forms of sexuality and even telecommunication centers for the lonely and the troubled. Elements of the counter-culture are continually absorbed and come of age.

Philadelphia is alive and well in these respects, despite the rigorous defense of older outlets and concepts. It is the home of the alternative school. The city's Parkway Program now has a thousand variations on its themes of self-directed urban education. Super Sunday, Olde City Sunday and yearly festivals along the Parkway are fresh responses to the continuing need for Philadelphians of all ages to get together and to celebrate life. The easy formlessness of these events—like the start of a high school dance—are part of the ongoing adaptive process.

A prerequisite to the flowering of healthy social groups and institutions is a human-scale, small environment in which the individual can achieve his or her balance. Sam Bass Warner recounts the unity of everyday life in colonial Philadelphia. The proximity of tavern, street, workshop and housing held the young city together in the eighteenth century. This ambience made it possible for merchants, artisans, shopkeepers and laborers to build accord and to define a common faith. It produced the close communication and later willingness to fight the war for independence.

One wonders if the Founding Fathers could have achieved their product in a city of two million. The Philadelphia of 2076 will need to provide a smaller, more intimate scale in order to permit satisfying and unifying transactions and associations to take place among its citizens. Colonial Philadelphia's size of roughly 18,000 inhabitants becomes a useful module for future planning. The rich, persistent presence of many such villages within the present fabric of Philadelphia still provides a basis for reestablishing this critical ingredient of scale. Every opportunity needs to be taken to strengthen their vitality in the years ahead, so long as free movement between them is assured for all the city's residents.

Reformulation of such a human scale will require that many functions of city government now managed and administered at a citywide level will, at greater dollar cost, be resumed under more local auspices. Other functions, however, such as sewers and water, will be ceded upward for efficiency's sake and because they are not heavily vested with conflicting value decisions, as are schools and health services. Under such a scheme, Manayunk, Germantown and Feltonville, along with Bala, Oreland and Marcus Hook will be the principal referents for Philadelphians. The government called Philadelphia will, like London, have spread outward to provide those broader services required by all. All its member units will be small, with primary functions to perform, but each with a distinct flavor. Unrestricted movement between them will be assured, today's sharp differences born of race and ethnic origin having been broken down through years of negotiation, legal action and growing personal opportunities for interaction and communication via school, place of work and on the streets of center city.

A slumless city—by current standards—will be emerging. Presently, abandoned areas will be reopened for settlement at reduced densities and with generous provision of open space and amenity. In presently sound areas, limits on materialism and demands for higher quality will place a premium on the rehabilitation of many existing homes and public structures. What are chic areas of center city for the upper middle class will have extended to the middle and lower income ranges of the city's residents. Banks and insurance companies will have incentives to assist in their renewal, rather than to hasten the process of abandonment.

The city's neighborhoods will come to look more like many European cities, where tidiness and reinvestment have replaced squalor and poverty. An acceleration of these developments will take place as these steps become fashionable and popular. TV programs will feature situations involving persons living in convenient and diversified urban life styles. Deliberate advertisements will be used to counter the remaining allure of outward moves. The next century will feature centripetal and recycling forces, well grounded in people's attitudes about the practical limits of the world in which they live.

Along with the physical changes to create a more human scale, new institutions will arise in the interstices between present systems, again on a small scale at first. A life-long process of continuing education will grow up between the current world of formal education and the world of work. Temple University's new center city unit, offering a wide variety of courses at all hours of the day and night, provides an early hint of what will be a growing industry. Midcareer shifts for men and women will be customary and not exceptional events.

Jobs for presumed unemployables, "superfluous people" such as exaddicts, exoffenders and gang youth, will grow up between existing places of work and points of rehabilitation and therapy. Such individuals work at a lesser pace and with some public support until they are able to enter the open marketplace for their proven talents and experiences.

New modes for satisfying Philadelphians' need for spiritual enrichment will grow up among the presently institutional churches, forms of psychiatric care, Eastern religious traditions and various secular institutions that now offer "outside help" for many seeking to understand the why of their existence.

The most difficult aspect of the future to envision is also the most crucial. What will the bulk of Philadelphians be doing with their time and talents by 2076? As hinted before, a major redefinition of present concepts of work will be taking place, again as seen in strands of thought now unfolding.

In addition to life-long programs of self-education, through which more and more people will come to follow two or more careers, a policy of guaranteed occupations will have been realized. Its justification will be the importance of maintaining the essential equilibrium of man, rather than merely the goods and services produced. Leisure, job and education will have lost their verbal and substantive distinctions. A new system of livelihoods will be evolving to replace both terms. Why indeed we do get up in the morning will have become the central theme.

Changed as well will be the present acceptance of dependency. The present welfare system will be gone and, with it, its marked contribution to the reinforcement of a sense of superfluousness in many individuals. A minimum income will be available to all Americans and be justified as a means of reducing antisocial, self-destructive behavior that is seen to stem from alienation and boredom and to represent a stupendous social cost.

The range of services that become useful occupations will increase many fold, especially in the human service field. Both at home, but also abroad, there will be an expanding market for the skills and experience of American workers, even then still relatively preeminent in the world. Today's advertisements for jobs in Australia will be matched by many newer nations in the world and will appear in the pages of the *Inquirer,* the *Bulletin* and the *Daily News.*

The concepts of the British economist, F. T. Schumacher, afford another constructive strand. "Middle level technology," the use of human labor in lieu of unnecessary technology, is a fertile field for adaptation to the rebuilding of the city. Expansion of labor-intensive practices is likely to occur in the wake of limits upon the use of new materials and the striving for higher quality, rather than the mere quantity of production. Middle level technology will grow as the doctrine of planned obsolescence is replaced. Its application is presaged in the growing ranks of artisans and craftsmen working in the recycling of older neighborhoods and the interest of the young in apprenticeships and careers in personally rewarding occupations.

Greater acceptance of labor-intensive activity and a new definition of the links between job and recreation will help to restore dignity to some occupations now deemed less desirable and prestigious. This effort could be advanced by status-building steps under established auspices. Philadelphia's colleges and universities might by then offer programs to teach craftsman skills in parity with training for the professions. Such a move would symbolize a shift in our thinking about the nature of work and would be reflected in the evolving economy geared to life in a more steady state.

A third avenue to solve the persistent lump of structural unemployment could be the concerted decentralization of many large institutions, private and public. Past moves to do so in local government have been resisted by the natural unwillingness of officials to relinquish power and control, but also because such moves are acknowledged to be more expensive. A monolithic structure is the cheapest one to operate in dollar costs; democratic institutions are the most expensive. Studies in the Philadelphia schools in the 1960's revealed that public education run on a district or neighborhood level would require more people and greater layers of superstructure to maintain necessary interrelationships. Greater communication and negotiation between more organized groups take additional time, money and people.

With personal health and equilibrium as emerging measures, such costs will be more readily accepted. Criteria featuring quality services and individual satisfaction will encourage such moves. Previews are observable in other cities, which have moved to concepts of local city halls and similar devices. Attainment of a crucial dimension of smaller scale will thus yield more satisfying roles for more people. Some of the costs incurred in creating such institutions will be offset by reductions in the costs of welfare and dependency, which now deplete governmental fiscal resources.

A far more complex variation on the decentralization theme would result from incentives to stimulate the redistribution of some population to smaller cities and towns beyond Philadelphia and its suburbs. Such efforts have been successfully managed in Western Europe, especially Holland, and may become feasible in the eastern United States as communication links become stronger and urban advantages are made available through time and space. Philadelphia medical centers now link their vast capacities to rural hospitals across the state to give diagnostic and back-up help via television.

Such ideas for generating new occupations and roles for future Philadelphians are variations on the more central theme of stretching our total resources in a post-frontier world. They are efforts to recycle the city . . . to budget in an encompassing world of man and nature with priority still given to the central role of the free individual. They accept the end of a throwaway society . . . both children and waste materials.

Philadelphia in 1976 already contains the seeds of an expanding recycling effort, despite the far greater evidence of deterioration and abandonment. The most easily recognized signs are evidenced in the old city where the Founding Fathers worked. From the most deteriorated and cast-off properties entire neighborhoods have been reclaimed. New economic values and higher qualitative standards have been created. While it can be argued that this has too frequently occurred at the expense of the poor, the more basic point is that the new and pleasing can arise from the old and decadent.

Building on its historic roots in this recycling process, Philadelphia has spawned dozens of small industries. Architectural firms, specialists in historic restoration and hundreds of contractors have become part of the recycling industry. The antique business is thriving and expanding. Salvage operations, marketing the residue from required demolition, have become remunerative and an occupation for many men. New professions are being created, and these include not only planners and inspectors who sometimes overabound in the recycling process.

Within the foreseeable future, large sections of residential Philadelphia will be impacted by the process of recycling. The kind of stability that has been steadfastly maintained in large areas of South Philadelphia will have been extended. Investors will be persuaded of the sense of this approach. Protection will be afforded to present residents, who will have first option to upgrade their present homes and neighborhoods. This recycling process will, before 2076, have steadily Europeanized the face of Philadelphia, often called the London of America. There will be a substantial offset to the process of abandonment that currently corrodes the city's quality of living.

Recycling applies not only to physical matters. The efforts of manpower development programs will be markedly expanded in the years ahead. OIC, already an international model for recycling personnel to do a variety of independent and satisfying jobs, was created in an abandoned police station whose use was itself recycled. Upgrading the environment of the city will place a premium upon individuals, the dignity of whose work will be more clearly esteemed by the public at large. If the recycling process catches on, there will begin to be real positions even for the retarded and the handicapped, based upon a realistic estimate of their limits but also the costs of failing to utilize their considerable potential.

The capacity for recycling within the city of Philadelphia is enormous, provided that the value placed upon higher qualitative standards is established first in personal attitudes and later in public policy. Ample evidence is at hand. Air pollution may be abating in portions of Philadelphia. The Schuylkill is again sustaining some forms of marine life. Tinicum's marshes still provide a home for ospreys and herons. Addicts and convicts are being rehabilitated and prepared to reenter the larger society.

Jobs and activities born of efforts at recycling are sustaining growing numbers of area residents in productive occupations. As the limits on our clocklike world of outer limits become better understood, new uses will arise for scrap, slag and other forms of waste. Streets and public places will receive new and better care and maintenance. Even human waste will be recycled to feed our lawns and gardens. The Japanese have done this for years; the city of Milwaukee's production of fertilizer by its sewer department has been successful for a generation.

The extent of the opportunity to generate both human satisfaction and income through recycling Philadelphia will depend ultimately upon the values that we define and hence the degree to which Philadelphians—en route to

2076—successfully adapt to living in a world of boundaries and the sheer necessity to conserve the common environment and to enhance the lot of their fellow citizens. It follows that active promotion and marketing of our newly discovered situation and its potentialities should be a major part of our planning for the future. It should be the hopeful note that is struck in the Bicentennial year.

CONCLUSION

This chapter closes without a rendering or a map of Philadelphia in 2076 or any year downstream. Hopefully, by then our major means of picturing Philadelphia will incorporate devices in addition to maps. A computer-derived reading may show where its citizens are in respect to health, education and other measures of well-being, as judged against the normal distributions of the bell-shaped curve. Distortions would be easily read and become the basis for corrective actions by government, both local and national. People, rather than land, will have become the central measure.

Philadelphia has extraordinary steps to take if such concepts for the future are to be realized even in part. There is certainly no guarantee that the city will succeed in making the necessary adaptations. Age-long battles with forces of destruction, jealousy, self-interest and the entropy of fundamental resources will persist. The period begins in a period of low spirit and personal insecurity. We are momentarily off balance as a nation and a city.

The turning point will come only if our society, in a place like Philadelphia, can develop a new, sustaining concept of our goals and purposes as individuals and as members of a larger society. Our greatest risk in adapting to the post-frontier world lies not in catastrophe, material shortages or world competition. These have threatened man before. Rather, it lies in any chronic acknowledgment that the individual's life has become cheap or absurd rather than precious and fundamental, as the Founding Fathers insisted that it was.

Hopefully, these pages have introduced some evidence that basic elements of the early American democratic faith can be successfully adapted for use in guiding the nation's next hundred years. That restatement begins with the replacement of a frontier outlook with one that forces us to stretch our resources, to utilize our capacity for rational activity as never before and to value anew the central role of the free individual.

FURTHER READING

This book is primarily one of interpretation about the life of Philadelphia. For readers who seek to inquire further into the city's past, present and future, certain books can be recommended. For the broad history of the city ranging from its foundation to modern times, the following are outstanding sources: John F. Watson, *Annals of Philadelphia and Pennsylvania in Olden Time...*, 3 vols. (Philadelphia: Edwin S. Stuart, 1905); Ellis Oberholtzer, *Philadelphia: A History of the City and Its People,* 3 vols. (Philadelphia: S. J. Clarke, 1921). A word of special praise must be accorded that great Victorian labor, the nearest thing we have to a comprehensive history of the city, the Thomas Scharf and Thompson Westcott *History of Philadelphia,* 3 vols. (Philadelphia: L. H. Everts, 1884). A shorter book dealing with the city is Sam Bass Warner, *The Private City: Philadelphia in Three Periods of Its Growth* (Philadelphia: University of Pennsylvania Press, 1968). A study that ranges across the history of the social life of the upper class of the city is E. Digby Baltzell, *The Philadelphia Gentlemen: The Making of a National Upper Class* (Glencoe, Illinois: The Free Press, 1958).

The reader who wishes to see how Philadelphia fits into the prerevolutionary urban context should consult Carl Bridenbaugh, *Cities in Revolt: Urban Life in America, 1743-1776,* rev. ed. (New York: Oxford University Press, 1971). The best general introduction to the Philadelphia of the period is Carl and Jessica Bridenbaugh, *Rebels and Gentlemen: Philadelphia in the Age of Franklin* (New York: Reynal & Hitchcock, 1942). Frederick B. Tolles, *Meeting House and Courting House: The Quaker Merchants of Colonial Philadelphia 1682-1763* (Chapel Hill: The University of North Carolina

Press, 1948) is also useful. Arthur L. Jensen, *The Maritime Commerce of Colonial Philadelphia* (Ann Arbor: Edwards Brothers, 1963) gives one a good sense of the city's commercial nature. David Hawke's *In the Midst of a Revolution* (Philadelphia: University of Pennsylvania Press, 1961) is especially valuable because it focuses on the year 1776. Richard A. Ryerson, "Leadership in Crisis: The Radical Committees of Philadelphia and the Coming of the Revolution in Pennsylvania, 1765-1776 . . ." (Ph. D. dissertation, Johns Hopkins University, 1973) is a valuable study of the politics of the day. (This work is available in most major libraries and in book form from the University Microfilms of Ann Arbor.) *Historic Philadelphia,* volume 43, Part 1 of the New Series of *Transactions of the American Philosophical Society* (Philadelphia: The American Philosophical Society, 1953) depicts the more "respectable" parts of the city.

Of special interest with respect to the Centennial period of 1876 is Dee Brown, *The Year of the Century: 1876* (New York: Scribners and Sons, 1966), as is John Maass *The Glorious Enterprise* (Watkins Glen, N.Y.: American Life Foundation, 1973). The social diversification of the city can be seen well in Allen Davis and Mark Haller, eds., *The Peoples of Philadelphia* (Philadelphia: Temple University Press, 1973).

For the contemporary city the following titles provide most interesting reading: Richard Wurman and John A. Gallery, *Man Made Philadelphia: A Guide to Its Physical and Cultural Environment* (Cambridge, Massachusetts: MIT Press, 1972); Peter Binzen, *White Town USA* (New York: Random House, 1970); Miriam Ershkowitz and Joseph Zikmund, eds., *Black Politics in Philadelphia* (New York: Basic Books, 1973).

Ruminations about the future can be aided by Robert Heilbroner, *An Inquiry into the Human Prospect* (New York: Norton, 1974); Barry Commoner, *The Closing Circle* (New York: Knopf, 1971); Rene Dubos, *A God Within* (New York: Scribners and Sons, 1971).

INDEX

THE CONTRIBUTORS

John K. Alexander is a member of the History Department of the University of Cincinnati and is a specialist in the study of the poor in colonial American society. He is the author of several articles dealing with the social life of Philadelphia between 1760 and 1800.

Dennis Clark is Executive Director of the Samuel S. Fels Fund, a public charity in Philadelphia. He is the author of several books on race relations and urban affairs, and in 1974 published a book on the *Irish in Philadelphia* (Temple University Press), a study concentrating on immigrant life in the 19th century.

Peter McGrath teaches at the Community College of Philadelphia and aided in preparing revisions of that city's Home Rule Charter. He is a widely known expert in political campaign management and an activist scholar in the problems of urban government.

Graham Finney is Director of the Philadelphia Partnership, a business and civic coalition working to improve Philadelphia life. He has had wide experience in city planning and in special programs to meet urban needs in a number of cities.

D4